UP ON HILL

Growing up in Post-war Parkstone

Paul McDonald

POOLE HISTORICAL TRUST
2011

This volume is published by the Poole Historical Trust whose primary aims are the promotion of research into and the publication of works on the history and life of Poole and the surrounding area.

Previous Publications

The Pride of Poole, 1688-1851

An Album of Old Poole

Mansions and Merchants of Poole and Dorset

Brownsea Islander

Poole and World War II

A Portfolio of Old Poole

Ebb-Tide at Poole

History of the Town of Poole, 1839 (facsimile)

The Sydenhams of Poole (booklet)

Art in Poole and Dorset

Victorian Poole

Poole after World War II 1945-1953

D-Day Poole (booklet)

The Spirit of Poole 1953-1963

Lifeboatmen Never Turn Back

Schools of Old Poole

Poole's Pride Regained 1964-1974

Poole Was My Oyster

Hengistbury Head - The Whole Story

I Was There

For Nature Not Humans

The Royal Motor Yacht Club 1905-2005 (private publication)

A Winsome Place

A Pint of Good Ale

Brownsea Island 1906 (facsimile)

ISBN 978-1-873535851

Prepared for publication by Terry McDonald.
Designed by Andrew S Arnold.
Production by Graphic Editions, Poole.
Printed and bound in Great Britain by Bournemouth Colour Press, Poole, Dorset.

Preface & Acknowledgements

I remember my childhood and teenage years in Upper Parkstone with great affection, the feeling of being part of a community, and having the liberty to roam far and wide in safety. For young boys (and girls) it was accepted as normal that they should enjoy a freedom that the children of today know little about.

The teenage trends through rock and roll, skiffle, and jazz, and the clothes, helped to make us what we are today. Duffel coats for the jazz boys, bouncing up and down in the sweaty basement of the Beacon Royal Hotel in Bournemouth. Drain pipe trousers and black trench coats with winkle-picker shoes for us rock and rollers and of course, made-to-measure suits from Burtons, in Poole High Street. For me, the dances upstairs at Branksome Conservative club and the Centenary Hall in Poole hold the best memories - no alcohol, just bottles of pop! And of course, the music and the girls! Plucking up the courage to ask a girl for a jive could be nerve-wracking but everyone enjoyed the last dance which was the 'creep'. No dancing ability needed, especially as the lights were turned right down. Just grab a girl and slide around the dance floor!

My friend John Hammond and I went to 'the pictures' at the Regal three times a week to pick up girls. In those days the programme changed three times a week - Monday to Wednesday, Thursday to Saturday, with another film on Sunday afternoon, so if you didn't get a girl there was always the film to watch!

As a C-streamer at school the thought of writing a book would have seemed impossible and my teacher, 'Killer' Hoy, would be amazed if he were here today! Some years ago I came across Patricia M. Wilnecker's Upper Parkstone books which I really enjoyed and are highly recommended. However, they only told the story to the end of the Second World War and did not cover 'my' period, the all important two decades following that conflict. A chance conversation with my brother (the academic in the family) about the existing books led to an agreement that he would offer his insights into the period and his skills as editor, if I could write it! It's taken a little while, but what you hold in your hands is the end result, UP ON HILL, and all I can hope is that it brings back a few memories and that you enjoy reading it as much as I enjoyed writing it.

Paul McDonald

Old Boy of Henry Harbin School, Poole 1952-1956.

Swanage, January 2011

Thanks to... My brother Terry McDonald and his wife Jenny, Allen Mabey, Ian Campbell, Ian McNulty, Mel Cox, Peter Smith, Mike Standhaft, Midge Holloway, Dave Guppy, Ian Woods, Hugh Woods, Keith Sloper, Billy Rudd, Martin, Adrian and Russell McDonald (my three sons), Megan, Emily, Cecilia, (my three granddaughters), Bournemouth Reference Library, Poole Museum, and Malcolm Collop, Andrew Hawkes, Mike Esau, Andrew P M Wright, Maurice Guy, Tony Hallworth, and the ladies, Andrea McDonald, Samanta Jelmini, and last but not least, my wife Vera. Without whose understanding and patience this book would not have been possible.

'Treburley' (now 87), Churchill Road.
The box room is the one above the front door.

Chapter 1

UPPER PARKSTONE
IN THE 1940s

Well, where to start? The day of my birth would be good I suppose! I was born on the 1st of August 1941 in Boscombe Hospital, Bournemouth, by Caesarean section. At the time most births would have taken place at home but my mother was 36 when I was born and (having already had a Caesarean two years earlier) the doctor insisted that she must have another hospital delivery. Bournemouth was then in Hampshire so my birth certificate gives that county as my place of birth but when, a couple of weeks later, I was taken home, it was to Dorset. As a child, growing up in Parkstone and going to school in Poole, I always wanted to be a child of Dorset, the county where I have, after all, lived throughout my life. In 1974, thanks to the boundary changes, my wish came true!

The home I was taken to was a modern, semi-detached house in Churchill Road, Upper Parkstone. There were four of us, my father and mother and my brother Terry who had been born two years earlier at Boscombe Hospital on the 15th August 1939. The house must have been almost new then, and it (along with a few others either side of it) did not have a street number. Instead it was named 'Treburley', presumably after a village of that name in Cornwall although we never found out why. Our answer of 'Treburley, Churchill Road' always puzzled our teachers when we had to tell them where we lived and probably confused a few postmen as well! It was eventually given a number and became 87, Churchill Road.

It stood on a flat piece of land, between Churchill Crescent and Livingstone Road, almost opposite the Post Office and General Store on the corner with Victoria Crescent. It was just before the big dip down into what we called 'Heavenly Bottom' and on to the 1 in 4 hill which led up to the 'Monkeys Hump' and into Rossmore. We had a fantastic view from our upstairs front windows, for although there was an old farm house with its yard and out buildings opposite us, we could look through the gap and could see Bourne Valley laid out before us, with the twin railway viaducts, and the steam trains passing by. Perhaps this was an omen of things to come! Our house had three bedrooms although the third one was really just a box room. My brother Terry had it as a bedroom until he grew too tall for it!

It was, of course, war time and our father was in the army, stationed at Bovington Camp. He had joined the army in 1937 and as a regular soldier, rather than a 'conscript', had somehow worked his way into what was probably a cosy job as a tank driving instructor. He was able to come home every night, and go back in the morning by catching a lift on the early milk lorry. My first memory of him is of me standing on a chair in the living room beside him, with him in his uniform and holding his rifle. Even though I was a war-time baby, I can remember little about it. Terry, being two years older, remembers some things such as Italian prisoners of war working in Churchill Road, presumably having come from the camp on Herbert Avenue. He also remembers seeing an occasional American soldier and gliders being towed through the skies on their way to Normandy in June 1944.

Our house, like everyone else's, had a strict blackout at night time and we had a metal framed 'Morrison' shelter in the back room which also served as a dining table. In the event of an air raid we were supposed to hide underneath it but neither Terry nor I have any memory of it happening. There were a number of air raids in the area with bombs destroying houses in roads within a mile or so of ours. However, neither of us can recall any bombed out houses in and around Churchill Road. I can, though, remember the demolition of the air raid shelters in Jubilee Road after the war and the caterpillar-tracked crane which had a large ball on a chain. The driver swung this with great aplomb into the rapidly disappearing structures and was very exciting for a small boy to watch.

The Churchill Road house was not my parents' first home for when they married, they lived in Sandford, near Wareham (because of its proximity to Bovington Camp) and then in a flat in Cranbrook Road, near Sea View. One Sunday lunch-time when my brother was a baby, Dad (who liked a drink) took him in his pram to the Sea View public house at Constitution Hill.

The Sea View Hotel, the scene of Terry's abandonment.

However, he came home alone and when Mum (naturally) asked him where the baby was, it dawned on him that he had left him in his pram outside the pub! Mum was not pleased but Terry has always been rather proud of being abandoned outside a pub at such an early age!

Dad became fed up with the (very) early morning trips to Bovington on the milk lorry and bought a motor cycle (a Vincent, I think) and I can remember rides up and down Churchill Road sitting on the petrol tank. He and his friend Herbie Bowden, another soldier, once raced each other home from Bovington, with Dad winning by the simple trick of going the wrong way round a roundabout as they were approaching Parkstone. I probably inherited my love of motorcycles from him.

Our mother was from Portsmouth and had moved to Bournemouth for work some years before the war. During the economic depression of the 1930s, the Poole-Bournemouth area was comparatively prosperous and one of her

Paul in the front garden of 87 Churchill Road.

brothers had already moved to Boscombe, working as a book-binder. She eventually became manageress of a dry cleaning firm in Bournemouth and had met our father at a dance at Bovington Camp, a year or so before the war. He was from Newfoundland which at the time was not part of Canada and had been a dominion in its own right. It had become bankrupt in 1934 and reverted to colonial status. Unemployment there was very high and Dad had sailed for Britain in 1937 on a ship carrying newsprint from the local paper mill, arriving in Swansea where he immediately joined the Army. It was to be another 37 years before he (with Mum) finally went back to Newfoundland and then only as a visitor to see his sister and other family members again.

Our mother's parents (our 'Nanny' and 'Noney') continued to live in Portsmouth until their house (which included the pawnbroker's shop that our grandfather managed) was destroyed in an air raid. It was in Queen's Street, in the heart of old Portsmouth and near to the Royal Navy Dockyard, a natural target for German bombers. After that, they moved to Parkstone, a much safer part of the world and at first they lived just three doors away from us in a bungalow on the corner of Churchill Crescent. Eventually they bought a house in Calvin Road, Winton where, in about 1947, they celebrated their golden wedding. This was a comparatively rare event in those days and the occasion for a large (Hitchins) family gathering. Terry and I were very impressed when their photograph, taken on that day, appeared in the Daily Echo.

As children our world centred around the cross roads where Churchill and Richmond Roads met the Ashley Road. Although we lived in Churchill Road we did not go to the local primary school, Heatherlands, as Mum had a low opinion of it and

Hants & Dorset bus at County Gates on its way to Poole.

somehow persuaded the authorities that we should go to Courthill School which was the other side of Ashley Road and reached via Richmond Road. Until we went to our secondary schools in Poole, much of our daily life was spent within an area bounded by Rossmore Road to the north, Bournemouth Road to the south, Alder Road to the east and Constitution Hill to the west. We often travelled outside of this area, of course, to Bournemouth or Poole, or to visit Mum's relatives in Winton and Boscombe or further afield but this would be with our parents. This usually meant our mother because after the war Dad had joined the merchant navy and was away at sea a lot of the time. He worked for both the Union Castle and Cunard lines and in post war Britain, with its rationing and shortages, his return from South Africa, New York, or the Caribbean, bring us all presents, meant that we became used to luxuries that our friends could only dream about.

The name Parkstone had originally been given to that part of the borough now known as Ashley Cross. It had grown rapidly in the early nineteenth century as people with enough money and leisure time began moving out of 'old' Poole to areas deemed to be physically attractive and, most importantly, healthy. By the middle of the century it was occasionally compared with glamorous Mediterranean resorts such as Mentone and its population was far more 'genteel' than Poole's other developing surburbs. As its population grew, so too did the concept of 'Parkstone' and it spread eastwards, past Constitution Hill and onwards to the Dorset-Hampshire border and the rapidly growing seaside resort of 'Bournemouth.' What became 'Upper Parkstone' and 'Branksome' developed as places for 'working' people to live, helped by the presence of local industries such as potteries. It was also halfway between Poole and Bournemouth and the coming of a tram service between the two towns in the early twentieth century meant that people had a reasonable catchment area in which they could seek employment.

Ashley Road looking east; a very quiet day for traffic.

By the mid twentieth century, our part of Upper Parkstone was a major shopping area and in those post-war days, there was a wide variety of different shops, most of them small family run businesses. The days of every High Street looking exactly the same had yet to come. As well as the main shopping streets, there were also the many 'corner shops' in the roads off Ashley Road and Churchill Road was blessed with many of these. In the half mile between our house and Ashley Road there were a number of corner shops selling basic groceries along with a post office, an off-licence and a fish and chip shop.

Opposite our house was the post-office and general stores run by a Mrs Gore and her sister and brother-in-law, Mr and Mrs Jelly who were originally from Swindon. They took over the ownership and running of the shop when Mrs Gore died. Mum shopped there every day, running a book which was paid up at the end of the week. As small boys we would try to obtain black jacks or penny chews on credit but Mr Jelly was more than a match for us and would send us away with a flea in our ear. I remember buying my first tobacco in this shop, half an ounce of Old Holborn and a packet of red Rizla papers and then going down to Branksome Recreation Ground and sitting in the bushes on the left hand side near to the long flight of steps that lead up to Playfields Drive. I was so sick that I thought I was going to die!

In the dip at the junction with New Road was a double fronted shop with an off-licence on the right hand side and general store on the left. The off licence was open in the evenings and did a steady trade in selling beer and cigarettes to the people from around the immediate area. Facing it, on the other side of the road, was the best shop of all, the fish and chip shop. I loved it when on a Saturday we had them for dinner (wrapped in news paper of course) with loads of salt and vinegar on mine. Mum and Terry were always fussy eaters and both hated the taste and smell of vinegar. There was another fish and chip shop up on hill, next to the Regal cinema on the corner of

7

Ashley and Jubilee Roads but that was a very old shop and closed in the late forties I think. They probably cooked them on a coal fired range as they were the best chips in town.

There seemed to be a shop on nearly every corner in Churchill Road, but my favourite was a general store on the corner of Buckland Road called Martin's. This shop, strangely, has lived in my memory all my life for the smell when you entered was just fantastic. Paraffin was the dominant smell, but cheese and ham and bacon were strong as well. The floor consisted of bare boards and a large wooden counter faced you on the right, the front being lined with biscuit tins and these had glass lids so you could see all the many varieties. On the corner of Norrish Road was a junk shop run by an old lady and this was memorable for the smell - it could really take your breath away when you entered it. Next up was another general store, and then there was Malmesbury and Parsons' Dairy. Our milk, though, was from the Co-op and Mr Blainey was our milk man and we used to help him on Saturdays or when we were not at school. Riding on his milk float was a top job. After Malmesbury and Parsons there was the Co-op Hall which was used for social gatherings such as wedding receptions and then the Co-op butchers and grocery departments. Mum worked as a cashier in the butchers, sitting in a little cubicle and taking the payments. The butchers were not allowed to handle the money so the cashier did it.

Ashley Road was always called 'up on hill' by people living in the roads either side of it and from our house it was about half a mile away and all the big shops were there. The largest was the Co-op (which is now The Parkstone Public House) and it was a department store. It had three floors and was in many ways reminiscent of the larger stores in Bournemouth such as Beales or Bobby's. Any shopping errand to the Co-op that we were sent on was always preceded with the words 'make sure you give the divvy number' meaning the membership number that entitled you to a small cash reward at the end of the year. Both Terry and I can still remember our mother's 'divvy' number to this day (it was 28402), 60 years later, such was its importance! I always remember this store because of its shoe department. It had a X-ray machine and this seemed fantastic to us as you stood on the platform, put your feet into the machine and looked down through the viewing hole where you could see the bones in your feet, and get a dose of radiation as well! But at least you knew if your new shoes were the correct fit. The store also had a large rocking horse to keep the children quiet whilst their mothers chose new shoes.

Further along Ashley Road, towards Bournemouth, was another large store called Butler's which sold linen and other household items. It was one of those shops that still had an overhead wire system for transporting cash from the counters to the 'office.' We always found this fascinating. Butler's had another branch in Boscombe which we would pass when visiting our Uncle and Aunt who lived in that part of Bournemouth. The other important shops in Ashley Road were a branch of Curry's (which sold cycles and radios) and a Woolworth's which seemed to sell everything. There were no checkouts in those days, just a large number of women or girls standing behind the counters who would take your money and hand you your purchase.

Perhaps the most imposing building was the Regal Cinema, which stood on the corner of Ashley and Jubilee Roads. In the days before every home had a television set, cinema-going was an immensely popular pastime with attendances in the early 1950s peaking at 1.395 billion people, six times higher than today. The Regal, like most cinemas, changed its programme every three days, and always had a newsreel and a shorter film to support the main feature. To us it was the place to spend Saturday mornings. For sixpence (downstairs) or ninepence (in the balcony) the Regal entertained hundreds of local children each week with a cartoon, a newsreel, a serial and a feature film, often the one that they were showing in the evenings. It was always extremely noisy as we cheered the good guys and booed the black-hatted bad guys in the westerns. Thanks to the Regal we were able to see the latest Tarzan or Roy Rogers' films although, on occasion, the plot of the film being shown went way over our heads. When this happened, everyone just talked to each other, so anyone trying to follow the film had little chance of understanding it! Saturday mornings at the Regal was our release to another world, namely America, and how I wanted to go there! I was in love with Doris Day.

For a while, in the early 1950s, we defected to the Grand Cinema in Westbourne, a relatively short bus-ride away. There was an added attraction in that there was a model shop next door to the cinema which sold balsa wood planes and lead soldiers. The Grand, as part of the ABC group, ran a 'club' for children on Saturday mornings called the 'ABC Minors.' You had to wear a badge, sing a silly song (We are the boys and girls well known as, Minors of the ABC…) and the films were always specially selected children's ones, so we eventually returned to the Regal and its more worldly ways. If there is one thing that shows how much the world has changed since those

The Regal Cinema, Parkstone, in the 1960s.

immediate post-war years it is that during the school holidays parents would give their children money to go to 'the pictures' in the afternoon and, if the main film had an 'A' (for 'Adult') certificate, rather than a 'U' certificate (which meant anyone could see it, whatever their age), we would wait outside and ask an adult to take us in. Someone nearly always did and I remember on one occasion a man taking about twelve of us waiting outside in to see the film. This practice would be unthinkable today!

At the crossroads of Ashley Road, Churchill Road and Richmond Road stood the pub that eventually became my Dad's local, the Retreat, a large and rather imposing building that had the Hants and Dorset bus garage behind it. On the other side of the road was St John's Church, another strong and imposing structure although I can never remember entering it. One of the stranger things about our parents was that Mum was a Strict Baptist and Dad was a Roman Catholic so, unlike all our friends in Churchill Road, we never went to Sunday School. We hated Sundays as there was no one to play with and there was nothing on the wireless that appealed to us. Our Strict Baptist grandparents, Nanny and Noney had (we were told) never entered a cinema or a pub in their lives, believing such places to be 'instruments of the devil.' Strict Baptists are, as the name implies, far more rigorous in their worship than 'ordinary' Baptists and can be likened to the Scottish 'Wee Frees' who lock up children's playgrounds on Sundays. After our grandfather died in 1950, Nanny moved in with us, and she used to go to a Strict Baptist chapel in Winton, being picked up in a car (very posh) each Sunday morning. Mum was never particularly religious although in her last few years she did attend Buckland Road Baptist Church quite regularly. The Retreat and St John's Church faced each other and it was always said that men coming out of the church on Sunday lunchtime would never walk straight across to the pub. Instead, they would cross Churchill Road, then Ashley Road and, finally, cross Richmond Road and enter the pub as if they were coming from a different direction. I doubt if it was true, but it was always a good story!

There were dozens of smaller shops along the Ashley Road and in its side streets but to me the best was Trinder's, the ironmongers. This shop was opposite Curry's and sold just about everything you could think of, and now, when ever I see the two Ronnie's famous 'fork handles' sketch it reminds me of that shop! Just along from Trinder's was (and still is) Branksome Conservative Club with a large dance hall upstairs.

There were also a number of newspaper and stationery shops along Ashley Road reflecting the massive sales that newspapers enjoyed in those days. Both the Daily Mirror and the Daily Express sold up to four million copies each day. We had the Daily Mirror and the Daily Echo delivered each day. Newsagents also sold children's comics with the Beano and Dandy being easily the most popular but because of the austerity of the times they were often regarded as unnecessary luxuries by parents so anyone lucky enough to be bought a copy each week would pass it from friend to friend. In 1950 a new sort of comic appeared and was an instant success. This was the Eagle and was clearly a 'superior' product, not least because its front page story was usually a Dan Dare adventure. Its centre pages were always given over to a highly detailed, cutaway drawing of an aircraft, or a warship, steam locomotive etc. It was far more educational than other comics but it did have slight religious overtones (there was always a Bible story on the back page), but as the editor was a clergyman called the Rev. Marcus Morris, this was probably inevitable.

Terry used to buy the Wizard and the Rover each week which were more like books than comics in that although each story had one or two illustrations, they were

Crewe's, our newsagent.

overwhelmingly narrative. He particularly enjoyed the stories about Alf Tupper ('The Tough of the Track'), a working class athlete who consistently beat the posh chaps from Oxford-type universities, despite existing on a diet of fish and chips and training late night around the cobbled streets of some grimy northern town. The Wizard also featured another imaginary athlete, the great William Wilson, who broke the world record in every event and, was inevitably the first man to run a mile in under four minutes. Interestingly, all of Wilson's feats, which were wildly implausible at the time, have now been surpassed by today's athletes. He also played cricket and his greatest achievement was to take ten wickets for no runs against the Australians when they had been set a target of just one run to win a test match. Even better, he defeated the world heavy weight boxing champion in 1832 and flew a Spitfire during the Second World War. A wonderful creation and if the dates mentioned look wrong it is because he had been born in 1795 and had discovered the elixir of life as a teenager! It was good, escapist stuff and he and Dad looked forward to collecting both comics from Crewe's newsagents each week.

Enjoyable as these British comics were, the real luxury in these post-war years were the American ones such as Superman, Batman, Captain Marvel and Classics Illustrated because they were clearly superior in content and production to ours and very difficult to get hold of. We were lucky, though, because with Dad being in the Merchant Navy and travelling to New York and back every two weeks, he bought a pile home after each trip. This made us very popular with other children who wanted to borrow them and we even had a man who owned a newsagent's shop on the Ashley Road come to our front door one day and ask if we had any American comics to sell. There was also a 'shop' run by an old lady halfway down the hill in Churchill Road who bought and sold American comic from the front room of her house. We were one of her best suppliers because of our steady supply of fresh material.

Back on the Ashley Road, along from the Retreat was Shepherd's cycle shop. This shop was important to me as all you could ever need as a boy mad about cycling was there. They had Raleigh, Hercules and Rudge cycles along with Claude Butler racing bikes and the Phillips' cycle speedway bikes. These had chrome front fork bracing and special low gearing for really quick get-aways out of the starting gate on the speedway track. How I wanted a yellow one!

Cycle speedway was a major sport for young boys in the post war years, mirroring the real thing for Poole Pirates had started in 1948. Some of the team's riders were among the biggest names in the sport and Ken Middleditch and Brian Crutcher both rode for England. Our local cycle speedway team were called the Parkstone Devils and raced at their track near Martin Road School which for some reason was always called the 'Cowsheds' by the children in the area. The track had been created on a piece of waste land by boys and their fathers and there was even a rudimentary starting gate. The Parkstone Devils were not the best team in the town, though. That honour went to the Oakdale based Gem Pirates who, in 1950, became the country's first ever national champions. There were other teams in the area, including the Newtown Eagles and the Tatnam Tigers and they all raced each other in organised matches.

After Shepherds was a butcher's shop called (I think) Yeate's, then another newsagent called Crewe's which was the one that delivered our newspapers to us. Terry had an 'Echo' round there, delivering the local evening paper six days a week for (eventually) 9s3d or 46p in today's money. Around the corner in Salisbury Road was the Liberal Club. Mum was a lifelong supporter of the Liberal Party and at election time she was always involved, with us boys used as runners. Dad always said he was a Conservative but as someone who had not been brought up in Britain, he was never that committed to any particular party and did not object to Mum using his proxy vote, when he was away at sea, to give the Liberals an extra supporter! In those days they certainly needed it for they seldom had more than six MPs in Parliament.

Next along was a garage they sold petrol over the pavement and also re-charged accumulator batteries. Mrs Cooper, our next door neighbour had her radio batteries charged there. Then there was another cycle shop but this one was much smaller and run by one man. He was the only person I have ever seen who could put a tyre back on a wheel rim with his bare hands - you avoid getting punctures that way. He also had a wheel-trueing jig, very useful for me as I was always in trouble with bent or buckled rims! Across the road was a fabric shop called Labett's and then a ladies' wear shop. Around the corner, in Mansfield Road and opposite the water tower was Aladdin's Cave, a shop that sold government surplus items. I used to buy my work boots there because they were ex-army and very well polished. On the other corner (Victoria Road) was a baby wear shop and they also sold Silver Cross prams which were once the ultimate transport for babies and the choice of the Royal Family. Today, with 'buggies' in universal use, Silver Cross seem only to make two types of prams, which tellingly are called 'Balmoral' and 'Kensington!'

Further along the road was Bob Foster's motorbike shop. This was a very large double fronted shop with an equally large workshop in the back. Bob Foster was a local legend, having been a winner at the Isle of Man Junior TT races in 1947, the first ones held after the war. He went on to become a world champion in the 350cc class in 1950. With a record like that he was obviously well respected in the world of motor cycling. Opposite, on the corner of Weymouth Road, was another newsagent and this one was called Biles. I did a paper round from here delivering a huge bag of Daily Echoes around Upper Parkstone. Biles' was well known to all us boys because it was the only shop that openly sold 'pin up' magazines. On its shelves were publications such as Spick and Span, Reveille, and Health and Efficiency, but they were not available for us young boys! Of course, by today's standards, these were very tame. Today's tabloid newspapers, such as the Sun's page 3, offer more titillation than those 1950s publications. Next along was the Methodist church, and around the back was the hall in Wesley Road that was to become an important place to me, for it was where the 3rd Parkstone Scout Troop met. Next door was the police station which included a Boys' Club at the rear of its premises. During my childhood a new police station was built further up the road, opposite Cranbrook Road.

This new station was just past the Parkstone Labour Club with the Woodlands Hall above it, the venue for many social occasions such as dances. Gerry and the Pacemakers played there in 1963 even though their hit 'I Like It' was already number one in the charts. Opposite the Labour Club was a monumental stone mason, Anthony Ives, whose the front yard was full of tomb stones and a fantastic life size angel that became a local land mark.

Westwards from here was the top of North Road which led down the hill to Park Gates and the Municipal Buildings and in doing so passed the most important place in our parents' social life, the Poole Ex-Servicemen's Club, which was later incorporated into the British Legion. I have fond memories of walking down to the club on a summer's evening. My brother and I always insisted on walking on the high wall that followed the pavement all the way down to the junction of North Road and Springfield Road. We liked doing it on our own without a helping hand from Dad and we always called it the 'High Pavement.' Dad would often take us to the club with him on Sunday lunchtimes. We were only allowed into the big room with two snooker tables or in the hall. Even poking our heads round the door into the bar was forbidden. One abiding memory of the Ex-Service club at the time was the many pictures of the battlefields of the First World War hung around its rooms. Stark and frightening, they depicted a very different world to then one we were growing up in yet were clearly relevant to a club

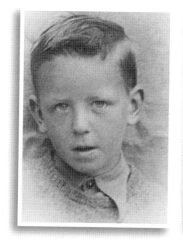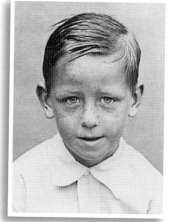

Paul and Terry.

Constitution Hill on a nice summer day.

Mum & Dad on a Sunday trip

for men who had served in the armed forces. Dad loved the club, remaining loyal to it throughout his life, serving on its committees and could usually be found there on a Saturday and Sunday lunchtime, holding court with his 'cronies.' He always maintained that at twelve o'clock on a Sunday he could hear the bolt on the door being slid back to open it up, despite our house a couple of miles away from it!

Carrying on from North Road was Constitution Hill, there was a large bus shelter here, and some buses terminated there (the No.5). Our gang frequently visited 'Con Hill' and we played around the water tower and in the tall pine trees that circled the tower. Climbing trees was second nature to us boys and we were like monkeys and dared to climb as high as possible and then drop to the ground from the highest branch some 20 feet from the ground. How we never broke our legs I don't know! Further on down the slope was a wooded area with secret places were you could have a kiss and a cuddle with your girl friend, and in fact my first fumbled fondle was there with a local girl whose name (sadly) I can't remember!

When the war was over and my father was demobbed, he went to work at the Wallis Tin Stamping Company in Hamworthy. I can still remember the smell of Dad's coat as he took it off and hung it on the back of the kitchen door, as we stood by hoping there might be some thing in his pockets for us! But Dad soon became bored working there and joined the merchant navy to see more of the world and I believe this was due to the wanderlust in his blood. Newfoundlanders have always been great travellers.

He started working for the Union Castle shipping line sailing on the Winchester Castle from Southampton to South Africa and he was away from home for six weeks at a time. But when he came home (for two weeks) a taxi would pull up out side our house, and we would run out to meet him. Dad would start unloading his suit case and sometimes brought boxes of apples and oranges, plus presents for Mum and us boys. In those austere times after the war and with food rationing still in place, bringing food like this to our door was amazing but there again our Dad was amazing!

Dad had been born 3 March 1913 on Fogo Island, Newfoundland at a small fishing settlement called Joe Batts Arm, but the family moved to the town of Grand Falls soon after, presumably for work. Grand Falls was a new town, created by the British newspaper owner Alfred Harmsworth, later Lord Northcliffe, in order to ensure a reliable supply of newsprint for his publications which included the Daily Mail. Harmsworth was worried that the fierce rivalry between Britain and Germany would eventually lead to war and severely restrict his access to European newsprint so, in 1905, he bought a million acres of forest in Newfoundland and four years later opened the new paper mill there. Our grandfather worked in this paper mill and Dad became a trainee fitter there. He was also a talented sportsman and played baseball and ice hockey at quite a high standard for local teams. As he once demonstrated when helping to fell a tree at his friend Herbie Bowden's mother-in-law's house in Vale Road, Parkstone, he could use a lasso as well! Surrounded by a crowd of local boys who could not believe that anyone in England could do such a thing, he calmly lassoed one of the tree's branches in order to help it fall. The local boys were astonished. We weren't!

Grand Falls in those days was very basic; although a big town in relation to others on the island it still had its dirt streets and wooden sidewalks. Dad would tell us stories of life when the snow came in the night and how opening the door the snow would be piled up against it, this meant digging your way out of the house and of course once the snow had arrived it stayed all winter long and you just got on with life. Both Terry and I longed to visit Grand Falls but this did not happen until we were in our fifties. Once there, we met literally dozens of our relatives, but it's still a small town.

In 1937 Dad and a friend decided to leave Newfoundland and 'cross the herring pond', as they called the Atlantic Ocean, and search for work in England. They sailed from Botwood in a small ship taking newsprint from the Grand Falls mill to be used by the Daily Mail. On arrival in Swansea docks, South Wales, he signed on and joined the army. He did his basic training at Catterick and then spent almost all of the war at Bovington camp as a tank driver/trainer. Towards the end of the war, he was transferred to Kirkby Steven in what is now Cumbria and we once visited him there, staying at a farm house where the farmer's wife wore clogs. Getting there meant an epic train journey for a mother and two small children, travelling all day across country in packed carriages full of servicemen.

Life as a small boy in Churchill Road was fun. We had no television of course, just an old valve radio, and I have fond memories sitting in the back room (we never did use the front room, that was for Christmas only) eating our bag of 'leavers' as we called the sweets left for us by our parents when they would spend an evening at the Ex-Service Club. We would sit in front of the coal fire with its light flickering on the ceiling and staring into the fire and seeing canyons and valleys in there while listening to Paul Temple on the wireless. I only have to hear the music entitled the Coronation Scot and I am transported back 60 years to that small back room in Churchill Road. Later, when we had a much better radio (a Pye), we scanned the radio dial for stations all over the world on the short wave with Morse code crackling in from some far off country. We marked those that we had picked up on a large globe of the world. We achieved the ultimate, I suppose, by once picking up a station in New Zealand.

A Grand Falls baseball team, c1935.
Dad is fourth from the left, middle row, with his hands crossed.)

Boxing was a major sport in those days and we would sit excitedly to hear Freddie Mills (a local boy, of course, and world light heavyweight boxing champion July 1948 – January 1950) or the American Joe Louis win yet another boxing match. On a Saturday we'd have to sit as quiet as lambs (as Mum would say), while Dad checked the football pools. At a quarter to seven every week day evening there was Dick Barton, Special Agent with his side kicks Jock and Snowy and just like every boy in the land, this was our favourite programme. I can remember Nanny (Hitchins) saying how pleased she was when it finished (all that violence you know) and a new serial called The Archers started. We wondered how long that would last! Terry always points out that there was another serial about a circus family called The Daring Dexters which lasted a few months during 1947 and occupied the quarter to seven spot between the ending of one Dick Barton series and the next. He's probably the only person to remember this!

In the corner of the back room was our Morrison shelter made of steel plate with wire mesh sides, it had a table cloth over it and was used as a table. Our gas masks were kept under the stairs. With a small selection of tools a hammer, a pair of pliers, a blunt hand saw, and a shoe tree (or 'last') used for shoe repair which in those days most families did themselves. We had chickens in the garden and also grew some vegetables and, despite the shortages and rather basic diet, we were very healthy.

We were among the first children to experience the benefits of what was to be called the 'Welfare State' and its centrepiece the National Health Service. I can remember Mum taking us to the Doctor's (Dr Devine, I think) on the Ashley Road and having to pay 2/6d for the consultation. This was probably in 1946 or 1947 as the NHS started in 1948.

We had the run of the local streets and we played games according to the season. It was football in winter, either in the road outside our house or down the road at Branksome recreation ground where we also played cricket, conkers, marbles and five stones (or 'dibs' as we called them), and hop scotch. This was marked out on the pavement with chalk. We also collected cigarette cards (or 'fag cards' as we called them), and played with our Dinky Toys and Meccano, (Dad had brought the Meccano sets home from South Africa as Christmas presents one year) often making covered wagons from the Wild West - Mum had to give us old pieces of cloth or handkerchiefs for this. All games were taken very seriously and played strictly to the rules.

Gypsies in "Heavenly Bottom", at the end of Albert Road, Parkstone, Poole. c1935.

Another pastime was digging 'camps' and we were lucky in that next door but one was what we called 'the field' (a empty building plot, really) and it gave us all the space we needed to let our imagination run wild. A camp would be dug into the ground and old corrugated sheets placed over the top then covered with turf. In the back corner of the field was the old, stone built, pig sty - the pigs had left long ago – and this provided us with a (roofless) base for our activities. We played cowboys and Indians for hours, and re-enacted all the scenes from the films we had seen at the Regal the previous Saturday morning. We also played down the hill in Heavenly Bottom and built dams in the Bourne stream. This was quite dangerous for us boys from the top of the hill, as the 'gangs' down there did not welcome us at all.

A favourite game of mine was rolling down Churchill Road to Heavenly Bottom, sitting on a narrow plank of wood fixed to a single roller skate. High speeds were possible if you could hold your nerve although there was a very high wear rate on the soles of my shoes. I would put a lot of effort into trying to ride a bike up the extraordinarily steep hill in Churchill Road from Heavenly Bottom up to Rossmore. I never did manage to do this for bikes in those days didn't have a low enough gear, unlike today when on a modern bike you can go up a mountain!

The Retreat Public House, Parkstone.

One summer evening 'Uncle' Herbie, Dad's best friend from his army days, picked us all up for a ride out to the country in his very old car. Herbie and Dad sat in the front, Mum and Herbie's wife 'Aunty' Barbara sat in the back and Terry and I sitting in the 'dickey seats' in the back i.e, in the boot well.

Once in the car, we set off down to Heavenly Bottom and up the 1 in 4 hill up to Rossmore only to stall half way up the hill! So Herbie let the car run back very slowly down the hill and upon reaching the bottom, he turned it around and set of up the hill in reverse with us boys laughing in the dickey in the back. We managed to reach the top of the hill this time and after turning around we set off again. I should add that in those days this hill was two-way traffic!

Owning a car was quite rare in those days but our parents were able to buy one from the money that Mum inherited when her parents died. It was not a large amount, but enabled them to buy a new three piece suite and a pre-war Austin car, registration number JPB 460. It brought a certain amount of freedom and we were able to go out for drives on a Sunday afternoon.

On the corner of Livingstone and Uppleby Roads there was a large reservoir half full of stagnant water. Left over from the war, this was great fun as the sides were a very shallow angle allowing us to ride our track bikes around it as if riding the wall of death good fun as long as you didn't fall in, which of course I did, and the got into trouble at home with Mum. But our bikes were our escape and we travelled far and wide. I remember riding to Wareham one day, to visit an old family friend, a man called Danny Bird who Mum and Dad had lodged with when they first got married. I remember in their back room or parlour, they had a coal fired range this kept them warm, as well as cooking all their food and boiling the kettle. Very cosy it was too.

I also remember cycling to Badbury Rings and back home through Wimborne. It was a very hot day and I was parched so I knocked on the door of a house in Canford village and asked for a drink of water. As a young boy out in the country side on my bike it seemed a quite normal think to do, I don't think they would open the door to you today! Canford Heath was also our playground and regular rides over the heath were common. Old Wareham Road was a dirt track in those days and I can remember seeing a tank driving up it once.

On a family Sunday afternoon trip to the countryside in Sunday best!!

Cuckoo Lane was at the top of the hill and Chalwyn Lamps' factory was opposite it. We loved all the bits of tin in the waste bins out side and tried to dream up uses for them but never did find one! Down Cuckoo Lane lived a relative of our next door neighbour, Mrs Trickett (I think she was her aunt), in a thatched cottage down the lane on the left hand side. In the garden was an orchard and beehives and this really was the most idyllic place I knew. But sadly it has now been wiped out as if it was never there! On over the hill was the junction with Oakdale on the left and on the right was the lane to 'Nut Wood', our main play area because there was a stream there.

At the start of the lane was the Gem Pirates cycle speedway track and then on through Nut Wood was a sand pit where we would dig up spent bullets and other small arms such as spent hand grenades and incendiary bombs. All very dangerous of course but not to us young boys – there was no 'health and safety' in those days! The track would then lead on to our main objective 'Hill 60'!

Local boys on old motor bikes would race up the hill to try to get over the top although in all my days there summer I never saw any one achieve this! The bikes were

Alexandra Park - Note the quality prams

old rigid frame models and they were unable to keep the front wheel down and usually did a back flip! We younger boys on our dirt bikes we would ride down from as high a starting point as possible daring each other to go higher, but know one ever did this. From the top there was a smaller hill called 'Hill 45' I think. It was not quite as much a challenge as Hill 60 but it was still an exciting ride! The long ride home meant I was always late and always had wet feet and torn trousers and would be in trouble with Mum.

We also rode to Longham bridge and played down by the river to catch minnows in our jam jars, and then maybe ride on to Hurn Airport to look over the fence at the aeroplanes. One I remember well was the De Havilland 'Dragon Rapide' bi-plane, painted in Royal Mail red and which took the mail to and from the Channel Islands.

But it was the school summer holidays that I remember best for it seems that the sun shone every day and six whole weeks was a lifetime to a small boy. Every chance was taken to go to the beach, and our favourite was Branksome Chine and getting there from Upper Parkstone was the best bit! This meant riding to 'up on hill', then across Ashley Road down

Paul at Branksome Chine, racing bike in the background.

through Alexandra Park along Bournemouth Road, down North Lodge Road, under the railway, across the junction at Penn Hill Avenue and into Branksome Woods. How we loved this place - the paths were fantastic, soft with pine needles, but criss-crossed by tree roots. There were two paths, the lower that followed the strong smelling stream and the high level that followed the boundary on the east side climbing up to a high level path and plunging down to the stream again, onwards through tunnels of rhododendron and over stone bridges on the race down to the sea. The woods were in six or seven sections, but divided by roads that crossed at ninety degrees to the path. About half way was a church set back into the woods, and across the road on a hill stood an ultra modern art deco house called The Conning Tower and we were all convinced that Dan Dare lived there!

A nice summer's day walk along the stream in Branksome Chine.

The last section of this path was more complicated and needed more skill or you would fall off.

The best part was kept until last when the banks of

The Channel coast at the end of Branksome Chine, note the boy standing on the 'Isle of Wight.'

the stream became a representation of the south coast of England, complete with the Isle of Wight which we loved to jump upon. The other side was meant to be the northern coast of France. All this stone work, paths, bridges and the sides of the stream were constructed by Welsh workers during the depression, I understand. On my lamp bracket on the handlebars was my towel roll with my swimming costume inside, and in my pocket was my dinner money. In hindsight we were all good (self-taught) swimmers and regularly swam out to the buoy that marked the sewer outfall a quarter of a mile out. One day we arrived at the Chine to discover a large yellow raft moored a hundred yards off the shore - this was just fantastic we now had some where to swim to and once there, to dive off. We would stay on the beach all day and then tired from the sand and sea face the long ride home at a much slower pace than in the morning.

In the winter, before Christmas, Bonfire Night was the big occasion although the first one I can remember was not just a Guy Fawkes celebration but one to celebrate the end of the war. This one was held at the end of Churchill Crescent, on empty land, where a large bonfire was built. I went with my Mum and Terry and all the neighbourhood was there. We had fireworks and jacket potatoes done in the ashes but unfortunately I got a spark down the side of my Wellington boots, and burnt my foot and had to go home early. From then on our bonfires were more modest affairs, held on the next door 'field' and organised by local boys with a little assistance form their parents.

Great planning went into the construction of the bonfire and most of the material came from Rossmore sawmill some two miles away, where Herbert Avenue meets Rossmore Road and opposite where the New Star pub now stands. Regular trips would be made up to Rossmore and branches too small to use for timber were begged from the mill owner. These were then made up into large bundles tied together and dragged through the streets with ropes back to our ever growing pile. We made up our 'guys' from old discarded clothes and stuffed with newspaper. Then, sitting in my go-cart, the guy would be taken up on hill to sit outside Curry's, and I would beg 'a penny for the guy.' This worked very well I seem to remember! All the money would be spent on fireworks, mainly 'bangers'. Standard Fireworks were the best as the different types were named after World War Two planes and bombers. Of course we all found this very exciting and the gap between finishing school and it getting dark enough for lighting the fire seemed to last forever, although it was probably only an hour or so!. Running around the dark gas-lit streets was what we boys did for entertainment in those post war years and letting of bangers in the street was all part of the fun. People seemed more tolerant then, I think!

We were friends with most of the boys who lived near us and among them was Terry Futcher who lived down the lane opposite our house. His garden was fantastic with large apple trees and a rear gate that came out in New Road. Steven Parker was another and he lived just down the road in a terrace on top of the hill that went down to Heavenly Bottom. We enjoyed making Keil Kraft or Veron's balsa wood aeroplane kits which hung from our bedroom ceiling suspended on cotton. I also smoked any dog ends we could find in his house and these would be stuck on a pin and smoked right down till it burnt your lips.

Malcolm Courtney was other friend and he was the youngest of three children whose name began with the letter 'M' - Mervyn, Mollie and Malcolm. Malcolm's dad had lots of sheds in their garden as I think he was a lorry driver, the sheds were painted with black pitch, and were full of wood and my abiding memory was that he had a hot glue pot which smelt terrible (animal bones I think). Next door to us lived Nigal Trickett (it should have been Nigel but apparently Mr Trickett mis-spelt it when registering the birth) and his sister Carol.

None of the houses around us had any form of heating other than the open coal fire in the back room. The floors were covered in lino or painted around the edges. In winter, draughts were a big problem so we had 'sausages' on the floor against the gap between the door and the floor or thick curtains hanging on the door. On very cold mornings there would be frost on the inside of the windows.

At night under the gas lights we would play 'tracking' with a piece of chalk - some one would be the hare and the rest of us would be the chasing pack. Chalk marks would be made on the street corners and after waiting the allotted time we would give chase. A favourite route was down New Road, up the hill and around Heatherlands School, (or 'Colditz' as we called it) down in to Cromwell Road over Churchill Road and in to Cheltenham Road, cutting through the little lane into Lyle Road and back to base outside the off-licence on the corner of Churchill and New Roads. I often wondered why it was called New Road when it contained some of the oldest houses and cottages in Upper Parkstone – pretty brick cottages with roses around the door and long front gardens. There was also a haulage firm operating in a large yard opposite.

Also in Churchill Road was a small garage called Churchill Motors up a side lane and Dad used to use this one and it's still in business today. Chubb's nursery was opposite - we did not go in there but preferred Turner's down on the corner of Uppleby and Livingstone Roads. On the other corner, opposite Turners, was Gardiner's, coal merchants, where we bought our coal. I can remember popping down to Mr Turner on a Sunday tea time just to buy a lettuce. A local character, Mr Turner, sold vegetables to the shops up on hill: he drove there on his motor bike and sidecar! Well, not really a sidecar but more of a wheel with a large wooden box on it. but it was the old house (Uppleby House) that fascinated us boys for it was full of old stuff, piles of old news paper, card board boxes and seed trays everywhere. In its old barn Mr Turner had a collection of old cars, one was a Rolls Royce I think! He also had old steam rollers. On the other side of the road was the orchard and it was in here that we spent a lot of our time scrumping, and making our selves sick through eating too many apples. My friends were Martin Gibbs, Jeff Williams, Brian Schooling and his dog called Mac! But watch out if Mr Turner got wind of your presence. You were in trouble because he could out run all of us, and if he caught you it was a clip around the ear. I often wonder if after spending all day bent over double, a chase with the local lads was not too much of an unwelcome distraction!

Our gang spent a lot of time in the woods lighting camp fires and eating under-cooked sausages. One abiding memory is that on the side of the woods that bounded Lawson Road lived a young girl who sat in the front bay window of her bungalow playing Diana by Paul Anka (1957) continually, while we boys tried to chat her up from our lofty perches in the trees over the fence. We also played on

Bill Turner

the roof of the school on the other side of the road for some reason that escapes me now!

The fair came to Branksome recreation ground every year, either Adlam's, or Coles. I loved going down to the fair and going on the rides, the swing chairs, the big wheel or best of all, the waltzer. This was the best ride for impressing the girls as the cars had a brake pedal and with a bit of skill you could hold the car back and then suddenly release the brake as the car swung around in a large arc. The juke box seemed louder on this ride! As well as the fairs, Billy Smart's and Chipperfield's circuses would visit Branksome 'rec' each year.

When I was eight years old, like many other boys of my age, I joined the 3rd Parkstone Boy Scout Troop, although at first I was officially a 'Wolf Cub' rather than a proper 'Scout.' We met each week in the Wesley Hall, part of the Methodist Church in Wesley Road and close to Bob Foster's motor cycle shop on Ashley Road. I loved the Scout movement and flourished within it. Suddenly I was good at something and I soon worked my way up to become a 'Sixer', the leader of a six-boy team within the Cubs. I loved the ritual and the practical exercises and games and longed to reach the age of ten when I would become a Scout. When my tenth birthday finally came, I took part in a ceremony where I was pulled over the line (a rope laid on the floor) by the older boys and I was, at last, no longer a Wolf Cub but a real Scout.

I continued to develop as part of the troop and proudly became Patrol Leader of the 'Wood Pigeon' pack. I learnt to tie complicated knots such as the reef knot, the sheepshank (for shortening a rope), the bowline, the round turn and two half hitches, and the clove hitch. Sixty years on, I can still remember how to tie them. We also played team games such as 'British Bulldog' and I always hated being on the losing side.

Our 'den' was opposite the scout hall and backed onto Bob Foster's. It was, in fact, our store house and was full of tents, pots and pans, and ropes but the main thing that caught my eye whenever we went into the den was an old 'trek cart.' There were many stories about the legendary scouts of the distant days before the war who, lacking any other means of transport, used the cart in order to go camping. I was determined to follow in their footsteps and lead the Wood Pigeons on a camping adventure using only the old trek cart.

Our local, permanent camp site was in Delph Woods, near Broadstone and some six miles away from our den in Upper Parkstone and the usual way of getting there was by way of the proper, tarmac roads. I had other plans. Looking at the Ordnance Survey map it seemed possible that we could get there by avoiding the main roads and cutting across the countryside. Thus with our loaded cart we went from Wesley Road towards Sea View, all along Ringwood Road until we reached West Howe and turned left at what is now the Clockhouse Garage. We plodded along gravel roads, following the old Lady Wimborne Drive and eventually came out in Arrowsmith Road. From there it was straight across the road and into Delph Woods, past Broadstone Cricket Club's ground and over a small stream to reach the camping field. Just how we managed to drag the cart all that way (and back, of course) I'll never know!

That 'adventure' was not the first time that I went camping with the Scouts. Each summer most of the 3rd Parkstone troop would go and I always looked forward to these trips with great excitement as they were the only summer holiday I would have. On the first occasion we only went as far as Chalbury, near Horton but in later years we went to Stratton, near Bude in Cornwall, and (in 1956) to Beer, in Devon.

3rd Parkstone summer camp at Manor Farm Chalbury. Paul is sitting on the tractor mud guard, wearing the hat.

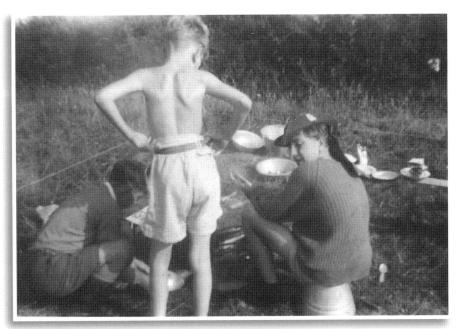

Summer camp at Beer in Devon. John Hammond (in hat) sitting on an upturned bucket

There were no creature comforts in camping with the Scouts, though. We'd pack the bare minimum in our ex-Army kit bag – a rubber ground sheet, a blanket and blanket pins, a change of clothes, an enamel plate and mug, a knife, fork and spoons. We'd also take something we never used, some soap and a flannel! All the gear, canvas tents, kit bags, huge pots and pans, were loaded into the back of a borrowed furniture van and all of us boys would clamber on top. We would sing songs such as The Happy Wanderer as we drove through the countryside but it would not be long before I felt sick, thanks to the motion of the lorry and the diesel fumes, and I would have to dash for the tailgate. But once arrived at our destination, the memories of the uncomfortable journey were soon forgotten. I loved to camp and still have very fond memories of those times. We never slept at all on the first night, spending the whole time laughing and telling jokes. When I arrived home from camp, after spending two weeks bent over a wood fire, I'd have to be fumigated by a disgusted Mum!

I made many friends during my time as a Scout including John Hammond who was to play an important role in my teenage musical career. Another was Ian Hunter whose father owned a butcher's shop on Ashley Road, close to its junction with Library Road. Mr Hunter was very keen on motor racing and, on occasion, I would be invited to go with him and his family to Ibsley in the New Forest to see the racing there. I loved the D-type Jaguars and the other 'top of the range' sports cars and the visits to Ibsley left me with a lifelong interest in all forms of motor sport.

Like so many other boys at this time, I was also interested in aircraft and the early fifties were, in many ways, a golden age for the British aircraft industry. Almost all the aircraft that were being designed and developed were British made and some of the test-pilots who flew them were household names. Neville Duke, who flew the Hawker Hunter, and Mike Lithgow with the Supermarine Swift both set new airspeed world records and were among the stars at the annual Farnborough Air Show in September. Terry and I went to Farnborough two or three times, travelling there with Cosy Coaches of Upper Parkstone. We were glad that we missed the 1952 show for that year one of de Havilland's test pilots, John Derry, was killed demonstrating a prototype DH 110, along with his crew member and 29 spectators. At home we often saw some of the new designs flying high above our house, including the mighty Bristol Brabazon and the Saunders- Roe Princess flying boat. The Princess was manufactured on the Isle of Wight and was one of a number of aircraft that were being built in the south of England. I remember the Airspeed Ambassador which was built in Christchurch and the Vickers Viscount at Hurn. To us, these were symbols of an enduring British success story. We'd won the war, we made the best cars and planes in the world and we still had an empire. What could possibly change?

It's a cliché to say that 'things aren't what they used to be' and I suspect that every generation feels the same about the world in which they grew up, believing it to have been a happier, less troubled time. The immediate post-war years probably seem so alien to young people today, but for those of us who grew up then, it was an exciting, optimistic and often joyful world.

Chapter 2

When it came to starting school, the strongest influence on where we should go was our Mother who came from a family with a strong educational ethos. Education had long been seen as the best means of social advancement for working and lower middle class families and two of her brothers had become teachers, one of them being Head of Modern Languages at one of Portsmouth's grammar schools. Some of her aunts, uncles and cousins were also teachers. Thus when it was time for Terry and me to start school she made sure that we went to somewhere other than the obvious one, Heatherlands in Cromwell Road, which was probably less than half a mile from our house. Somehow she knew that it wasn't that good a school and as Terry was later to point out, during his five years at Poole Grammar School, he never came across a boy who had been at Heatherlands. On the other hand, in 1950, the year he passed his Eleven-plus examination, he was just one of seventeen boys from Courthill School to go to the Grammar School, and there were probably a similar number of girls who went from Courthill to Parkstone Grammar School that year.

Although we were unaware of it, we started school at a time when great changes were being made to education in Great Britain with Parliament passing the 1944 Education Act. For the first time all state education was free and (in theory) a child, whatever his or her background, could climb as high up the career ladder as their abilities would take them. In reality, because of social constraints, only a minority of children were able to take advantage of this new opportunity but for that minority it was certainly the making of them.

I started school at a very young age, three I think. This was far too early and it was probably a result of both of us being August babies which meant we would nearly always be the youngest in the class. I went to Courthill Infants in Courthill Road, Lower Parkstone, where Terry had started a year earlier, when he was four. We would walk with Mum the mile or so there and the same coming back in all weathers, quite normal in those days, unlike now with children delivered to school in huge 4 x 4s, regardless of the weather.

Courthill School was really two schools, the Infants' and the Primary, with the latter usually referred to as the 'Big School.' Each had a different head teacher and although they shared a 'campus', each had its own buildings and playgrounds. My first

Paul (second from right, third row) at Courthill Primary (the 'Big School') – Mr Fry the headmaster is on the right. There were thirty three children in the class.

Paul at primary school

memories of the Infants' School are queuing for cod-liver oil every day and going to bed in the afternoon on small camp beds which were set out in rows in the school hall.

The Infants' School Headmistress was Mrs Taylor and she said I had a nice singing voice! The songs we sang included Greensleeves, The Minstrel Boy and The Sweet Lass of Richmond Hill. I enjoyed singing but how I struggled at the academic subjects. Luckily I enjoyed sports and one activity was country dancing, something we seemed to do at every opportunity. Dancing around the playground with our coloured braids crossed over our cardigans and pullovers, all this energy culminating in the annual county display at Bovington Camp.

I longed to go up to the 'big school', (the primary) and I remember looking through the cast iron railings in the front playground that separated the two schools. However, when the day came to 'go up' I did not cope very well at all and my abiding memories are of sitting at my desk and crying a lot at my inability to understand basic maths, spelling and reading. It was because of this that I was kept back a year until I could read to a reasonable standard. I was then put back in to the correct class for my age but I had, of course, missed a year of schooling and had no idea what the teacher was talking about , and was teased for this. Our surname was also a source for teasing as other children would sing that old favourite Old MacDonald had a Farm (which I hated) in our presence. The main event of the day was dinner time, I always enjoyed school dinners, even tapioca which we called 'frogs' spawn.'

One unusual feature of Courthill School at this time was that it experienced an influx of children from outside its obvious catchment area. Although Terry and I lived on the 'wrong' side of the Ashley Road for Courthill, these new children were from Oakdale, much further afield. Their presence at Courthill had been brought about by the urgent need for housing in the immediate post-war years and the subsequent

Terry (second left, second row) at Courthill. The teachers are Mr Davidge (a student teacher at the time, who returned to the school as a full time teacher and I believe eventually became Head Master) and Miss Penney who taught Class 1. There were 38 children in the class.

Very smart with my I-spy badges

building a new council estate in the Oakdale area. As Courthill School apparently had plenty of room, they were brought in on two double-decker buses each day. My friend Midge Holloway was one of these children, and I still see Midge today!.

Courthill School's head master was Mr Fry, a man who was (for those days) very forward thinking in his teaching methods and a new lesson was introduced that taught us all about the environment and the natural world. We enjoyed this because it meant going out into Alexandra Park to study the trees and plants. There were only eight classes for the four year groups with the odd numbered ones (1,3,5 and 7) being (unofficially) for those expected to pass the 'eleven plus' examination and go on to the town's two grammar schools. The 1944 Education Act had created three types of schools – Grammars for those deemed to be 'academic', Technical Schools for those deemed bright but with an aptitude for practical, scientific subjects and Secondary Moderns for everyone else. Only a few boys – it was always boys – went to the Technical School in Weymouth. To get there each day they had to travel by train. Very adventurous!

Mr Fry also taught that was, to many children, the highlight of the school week, a lesson called 'Great Lives' when the two classes for each age year were combined and listened to him tell us all about the famous historical figure whose picture he had pinned up in front of us. Through this simple idea we were made aware of the roles played in the shaping of the country (and the Empire) by people such as Sir Francis Drake, Sir Walter Raleigh, Clive of India, Florence Nightingale, Lord Nelson etc, etc.

I always enjoyed the School trips and particularly remember going to Bristol Zoo, and to Longleat House. We travelled in coaches hired from two local companies, Charlies' Cars of Bournemouth and Cosy Coaches whose offices and garage were on the Ashley Road, near Branksome Library.

Another school trip, probably when I was at Henry Harbin, was to The Bath and West Agricultural Show which one year was held on Magna Road, near Bear Cross. This was the first time it had been held in Poole and it later moved to a permanent home at Shepton Mallet. I also remember a trip round Ryvita's factory in Upper Parkstone. One summer we went camping with our teacher Mr Davidge to Tarrant Keynston where we erected our tents in a field behind the car park of the pub, the True Lovers' Knot. This was great fun and was my first time away from home we stayed

there for 2 weeks. We created a temporary shower utilising a dustbin. I think we walked into Blandford and also played in the stream that meandered through the Tarrant Valley, below Tarrant Rushton air field. But sadly I had very bad toothache during this 'holiday' and had to go home and go to the dentist. I managed to return to the camp for the last days. I loved camping and it was soon after this that I joined the cub scouts or the Wolf Cubs as they were called then.

At the end of each summer term Courthill School had its own sports day with races in the road

Group picture of summer camp with Mr Davidge.

outside the school although the proceedings had to stop if a car coming along the road. Fortunately, these interruptions only happened two or three times in an afternoon. There were also the annual gymnastic displays in the lower playground, and I enjoyed taking part in them. We performed complicated tableaux, but the highlight for me was when I had to dive through a paper hoop. However, on one occasion, I fell as I landed causing much commotion from teachers and parents and I was carried away on a stretcher.

Home made shower.

The Poole area schools' sports day was always held at the Gas Works sports ground at the junction of Alder Road and Yarmouth Road. This large sports field, complete with 'grandstand', was the home ground to the Bournemouth Gasworks Athletic Football Club, a top team in their day - the call from their fans was 'up the Lights!' They had been the

General view of the camp site.

School gymnastic display team.

Boys from Parkstone Sea Training School up the mast in front of the school.

losing finalists (1-5 to Ilford) in the FA Amateur Cup competition in 1930 and, twenty years later, were still remembered in and around the town for this achievement. All the Poole schools were represented at the sports day and a march past the large grand stand with the best athlete holding the school name up high on a placard.

A school that always impressed was the Parkstone Sea Training School, run by the Dr Barnado Organisation. It was in Constitution Hill Road and its building is now part of the Bournemouth and Poole College of Further Education. The land at the junction of Ringwood Road and Constitution Hill Road, now a Day Centre, was their playing field. Their uniform was so plain and austere - lots of cold showers there I think! On the town's schools' sports day, the competition was fierce and so we all ran, jumped and hopped and skipped for the honour of our school.

It was around this time that my brother told the school the reason I was not learning was that I was deaf! He had taken seriously our mother's occasional comment of 'that boy's deaf' when I wasn't listening to something she'd said! This caused the school some concern and Mum had to take me to see a specialist at the Municipal Buildings at Park Gates, Lower Parkstone, but after exhaustive tests on my hearing, I was pronounced normal. The real problem was that I was dyslexic, but unfortunately this was not a recognised condition at that time. It was thought that I was just stupid!

I enjoyed the practical subjects and on one occasion we made cardboard models of the new Poole power station at Hamworthy. The 1951 Festival of Britain was a major event at this time and we made models of some of its best known features such as the 'Skylon', the 'Dome of Discovery' and the 'Shot Tower.' A French exchange student made a fantastic model of the 'Skylon!'

When I was ten, King George VI died (February 1952) and this was announced in the playground to all of the school. At Poole Grammar, Terry's class was called in from the sports field and they were told the news in the changing room. A long period of official mourning began with only dirges on the radio and the newspapers edged in black. It felt very strange having to sing 'God Save the Queen' rather than 'King!'

Another place I seemed to visit far too often at that time was the school dentist in Shillito Road. This was located in the old Branksome Urban District Council offices, a large and imposing building on the corner with Library Road which today is Bob Hann House, a 'pop-in' centre for Age Concern. The dentist's surgery was upstairs in a wood panelled room and while sitting in the waiting room you could here the cries of the poor victim and also the drill doing its work! I have very bad memories of many extractions, and all by the dreaded gas! The smell of that rubber face mask gave me nightmares as he held it over my face. I used to dream of a little red man on a motor

The Grandstand at the Bournemouth Gasworks Athletic Football Club's ground.

cycle buzzing around and around on the wall of death, but going faster and faster until it turned into a scream. I suffered from toothache a lot, but of course at home if I had loose teeth they were pulled out by cotton tied to the door handle and the door slammed. Toothache at home was also treated with oil of cloves which made your mouth go numb.

Like many children at this time, I used to suffer from boils a lot. Mum would treat them with a kaolin poultice, an evil mixture that was heated up in its jar, put into a saucepan of hot water, spread on a lint pad and then placed on the boil as hot as you could tolerate it. This made you jump and cry out in pain as you waited for the pad to cool down and draw out the pus. Boils always left a scar. The largest one I had was on my knee, the result of several small boils that had come together to form a large carbuncle – I still have the scars to this day! Ear-ache was treated with olive oil with the bottle being put by the fire and when it was warm the oil was pored in to your ear which was then plugged with cotton wool. Cuts were treated with Germolene ointment, and sunburn with calamine lotion. You were careful not to swallow hair or you will get

Henry Harbin School.

a hair ball in your stomach and to make sure you did not cut your hand between the thumb and first finger in the vee, as this would give you lockjaw! Also, as all the children in Churchill Road knew, standing over a drain would give you scarlet fever!

A big test for me was the 'eleven plus' exam that Terry had passed two years earlier, on 17 March 1950, the day of our (Hitchins) grandfather's funeral. Two years later it was my turn and I remember going to Poole Grammar School, next to the Ladies' Walking Field, to sit the exam. I sat there looking at the test papers in a daze and hurriedly writing down the first thing that came into my head (all misspelt of course) with the inevitable result, I failed.

There were five schools in Poole for children when they reached the age of eleven. The two (single sex) grammar schools, Kemp Welch in Rossmore, Herbert Carter in Hamworthy, and Henry Harbin in Poole. These last three were designated as 'secondary moderns' and, like the grammar schools, taught boys and girls separately but shared campuses.

As expected, I failed the 'eleven plus' and was sent to Henry Harbin School in Poole! What was a boy from Upper Parkstone doing going to a school in Poole you might well ask. Well, it was another example of Mum beating the system. Her prejudices against Heatherlands were nothing to her attitude towards Kemp Welch School, which was where all the children around us went to. Kemp Welch School was situated on Herbert Avenue and was surrounded by a number of the new council estates that had been hurriedly built after the war. It had a reputation for poor academic standards and lax discipline and our mother was adamant that we would never go there. There was the added factor that it was always said that pregnancies were commonplace among the girls there so to protect my innocence she managed to arrange for me to go to Henry Harbin rather than Kemp Welch!

Of course all my friends in and around Churchill Road went to Kemp Welch and I was told that my name was called out at that school's first morning assembly. I, of course, was already in Poole. This was not as bad as it might seem because having gone to Courthill School, I had many friends there (who mostly lived in Lower Parkstone), and as they had also failed the eleven plus, they too ended up at Henry Harbin.

Mum had, of course, insisted that I had the full school uniform - cap, blazer, short trousers, tie, gabardine mac, and new shoes for winter and sandals for summer. So smart was I that I was frequently called into the office of Mr Smith, the headmaster to show the parents of new boys what the proper uniform looked like. Not many others wore it!

I rode my bike to school every day in all weather, rain or shine. It was easy going to school because it was all downhill but coming home was another story for it was up hill all the way! On the way to school I would call into the sweet shop by the side of the Centenary Hall and buy penny chews or black jacks. Along the road, on the other side, was a shop called 'Unique Stores' which sold absolutely everything, all of it very cheaply. In fact, no one could sell it cheaper.

My first form master was 'Gandy' Roberts's, a teacher from the old school who took great pleasure in inflicting torture on us boys. His favoured trick was to hold you by the ear and flick the lobe, he was an expert at this and could cause great pain. He also had a superb talent with the cane which he used at every opportunity. He also kept all the canes for the rest of the school (or so it seemed) in the cupboard under the blackboard and there were always boys knocking the door to collect a cane for teacher, presumably to be used on themselves. But for me the main attraction was looking out of the window at 9.55 and watching the Pines Express make its storming departure from Poole Station with a standard '5' on the front, and a twelve car rake of 'Midland red' carriages. It had destination boards on the gutter side marked, Bournemouth to Manchester! Manchester? Where on earth was Manchester, I wondered! And dreaming that maybe one day I could be on the engine's foot plate! All the way to God knows where!

My four years at Henry Harbin were spent in the C stream with Years 2, 3 and 4 being in the care of a teacher known as 'Killer' Hoy. 'Killer' was a Canadian, like my father, so we got on quite well. We even played baseball rather than rounders as I had a catcher's mitt that Dad had brought back

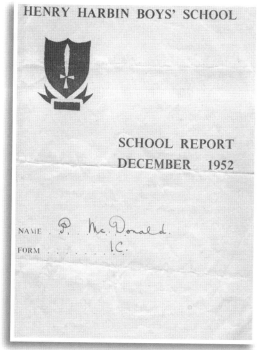

HENRY HARBIN BOYS' SCHOOL

SCHOOL REPORT

DECEMBER 1952

NAME . P. Mc Donald.

FORM . . . . 1C.

School report from "Gandy" Roberts

Poole station approach in early 1960's.

from one of his trips to America so we called our team the Canucks! He drove a black 'sit up and beg' Ford Popular and my job in the winter was to put a paraffin lamp under the engine to stop it from freezing up. He also kept an old coat under the bonnet on top of the engine - winters seemed colder in those days. I used to help him run the school film shows, and remember taking the films for return over to Sterte Post Office, across the footbridge over the railway where I always lingered in case a train should pass underneath.

The school day started with assembly in the playground and we lined up in our classes, standing upright and ready for inspection by the deputy head, Taffy Philips. I would frantically rub my shoes on the back of my socks to put a shine on them! Then we filed into the hall for morning assembly to stand and pray to the Lord and sing a hymn.

I was still useless at maths and English and I continued to struggle with schooling. However, I did enjoy history and geography and also the practical subjects such as pottery, woodwork and metalwork. Mr Jenkins was the metal work teacher and was a strict disciplinarian – he once caned the whole class, some 40 boys (!) one dinner time for straying in to the girls' playground. I remember that he couldn't pronounce nought and used to say ought. I also remember some one accidentally knocking down a girl one dinner time and she fell down rather heavenly and broke her femur. We all felt terrible about that at the time.

One thing that I did excel at was cross-country running and our team came first in Dorset Schools Athletic Association's secondary championships at Lyme Regis in March 1956, but I hated track running! Terry was a good runner, winning the Grammar School cross-country championship one year and becoming Poole Schools mile champion in 1955. Like my brother, I eventually joined Bournemouth Athletic Club and ran in cross country races for B.A.C. with modest success. We had to travel across

Bournemouth Athletic Club's Cross Country Team c1956. I am in the middle, front row and Terry is second from the left in the back row. One of Bournemouth's great characters, Ken Baily, is on the right of the club's president, Charlie Paulding, in the middle row.

Bournemouth to the Linden Hall Hotel in Boscombe on training evenings and we would run along the sea front and up and down the zig-zags. The evening would end with a swim in the hotel's pool.

I remember the whole school going to the Regent cinema to see The Ascent of Everest in 1953 and also a trip to the Pavilion in Bournemouth to see Shakespeare's Richard the Third . Other activities include swimming which took place in Poole Park, at the open air baths in Park Lane, next to the railway line as it traversed the boating lake. We visited the baths often, culminating in the annual inter house swimming competition. I was in Joliffe House, so if you could swim then you were in it! Sadly the baths are no more but I can still remember the boys' changing room with its wet and slimy floor. A good place to catch polio I think! In the 1950s swimming baths were frequently regarded as places where that disease lurked.

On the whole, I did not really enjoy school and when I was approaching fifteen I was glad to be leaving. I had enjoyed the practical subjects and with hindsight, I wish I had been able to go to the Technical School in Weymouth. As it was, in the summer of 1956 (still only fourteen years old) and like so many others at the time, I left with no formal qualifications and no clear idea of what I wanted to do.

A brand new Poole swimming baths, looks like it's being filled for the first time!

The opening of the new Poole swimming baths.

Chapter 3

MUSIC

The first music I can remember hearing was Mum singing hymns, joining in with radio programmes such as Sunday Half Hour. She had a lovely alto voice and used to proudly tell us that she'd won a prize for singing when she was a young girl in Portsmouth. Her family, the Hitchins, were quite musical and when our grandmother (Nanny) lived with us she had a small (actually, it was quite large!) organ in the front room but Mum seldom, if ever, played it although she could play the piano, as long as she had the sheet music in front of her. One of her brothers was also a very good pianist and organist, writing and producing musical shows at the school in Portsmouth where he was a teacher.

For us, most of the music that we grew up with came from the radio (or 'wireless' as everyone called it) and in our house it was on continually. Nearly everything we listened to came from the BBC of course and it had just three channels at this time, The Home Service, The Light Programme and The Third Programme. The first of these is now Radio Four, the Light Programme is Radio Two and the Third programme is now Radio Three. We'd listen to the Home Service some of the time, mainly for the plays on Saturday Night Theatre, and Children's Hour everyday at five o'clock but it was the Light Programme (now Radio 2) with its music, panel games, serials such as Paul Temple, variety shows and comedy shows that was our normal listening. 'Take It From Here' was a firm favourite and for Terry and me, the adventures of Special Agent Dick Barton and his two assistants at a quarter to seven every weekday evening was unmissable.

The worst day of the week for radio entertainment was Sunday for although there were music programmes such as the Billy Cotton Band Show (Wakey, Wakey!) with the band's resident singer Alan Breeze performing silly songs such as I'm a Lonely Little Petunia in an Onion Patch. Much of the Light Programme's output was intended to gently improve the cultural standards of the nation. One such programme, on a Sunday afternoon, was called 'Down Your Way', and its presenter (usually an important figure from the BBC establishment such as Richard Dimbleby or Franklin Englemann) would visit a small community or institution and talk to the people living or working there. Each interview would end with the host asking them to choose a piece of music to be played on the programme. Even the most humble of interviewees, such as a gardener at a stately home, would always chose a classical piece which seemed strange to us for we never listened to the Third Programme and never met anyone who did! It was probably another case of the BBC producers trying to 'improve' the musical tastes of an audience that preferred 'dance band music.' This form of music, though, was 'rationed' and there were a surprising number of slightly 'highbrow' programmes, even on the Light Programme. Friday Night is Music Night (which began in 1952 and is still running) is a good examples, and we would inwardly groan on a Sunday evening when the very polite BBC announcer would tell us that 'we are now going straight through the glass doors into the Palm Court of the Grand Hotel' where Max Jaffa and a string orchestra would be waiting to play for us. The 'Grand Hotel' was actually in Scarborough and the violinist Max Jaffa led the 'Palm Court Orchestra.' Terry admits to having once seen the Max Jaffa Trio in concert at Bournemouth's Winter Gardens.

Many of its programmes such as Two-Way Family Favourites on Sunday lunch time were music based and I can still remember many of the songs from that time. I suspect many people who were young in the post war years remember the music of the era as being pretty bland and there were a surprising number of 'novelty' songs featured on the Light Programme. There was Sparky and his Magic Piano and The Three Billy Goats Gruff (I'm a troll, fol-de-rol...) and many American records by artistes such as Phil Harris (Woodman, Woodman Spare That Tree) and Bing Crosby. This last singer was immensely popular in Britain and Dad's friend Herbie Bowden could do a very good Bing Crosby impression, so good that he even auditioned for the Carol Levis Discoveries show for the BBC. Canadian born Levis would tour Britain seeking talent to feature on his radio show. Good as we thought he was, Herbie didn't get through the audition.

There were signs of change in the early fifties with the coming of the more 'modern' Americans such as Frankie Laine, who sang I Believe and Johnny Ray with Cry and The Little White Cloud that Cried. Among the big instrumental hits of the late 1940s was the Harry Lime Theme, a piece of zither music from the hit film The Third Man. The biggest British singing star was the crooner Donald Peers whose weekly radio show (from 1948) attracted huge numbers of listeners and was characterised by the near hysteria from the young women in the audience when it was being recorded. Mum was a fan of his.

Although the BBC had a monopoly of broadcasting in Britain there was an alternative, albeit a foreign one. Radio Luxembourg ('208 on the medium wave') was to us rather exotic because it included advertisements, but its real attraction was its emphasis on the popular music of the day. On a Sunday evening it had a 'hit parade' programme called 'The Top Twenty' that was based on record sales rather than sheet music. It was required listening for everyone interested in 'popular' music, which was probably everyone we knew. A curious legacy from the days of Radio Luxembourg is that most people of a certain age who hear the town of Keynsham, near Bristol, mentioned will automatically spell it out – K.E.Y.N.S.H.A.M......This is because Radio Luxembourg would play an advertisement for Horace Batchelor's apparently fool-proof method for winning the football pools, his 'infra-draw' system, seemingly between every other record. 'Keynsham' was where you were urged to send you postal order and always spelt in full. It entered the nation's subconscious memory!

We were a musical generation in that we all loved music especially the 'big bands' that played regularly at the two main venues in Bournemouth, the Winter Gardens and the Pavilion. The leaders of these bands, or 'orchestras' as they preferred to be called, were household names and Terry (being two years older than me) saw them all - Ted Heath, Johnny Dankworth, Jack Parnell, Ken Mackintosh, Eric Delaney and many others. Even the popular solo singers of the day (on both sides of the Atlantic) had usually begun their careers as singers with such bands.

At this time, a long running dispute between the British and American Musicians' Unions had meant that no American band could play in Britain (and vice versa) but in the mid fifties a compromise was reached. This was to allow an American band to come and play in Britain while a British band went and played in America. The first instance of this happening involved the Stan Kenton Orchestra and Terry saw them when they played at the Winter Gardens in 1956. A number of famous American bands followed Kenton and came to play in prestigious concert halls whilst their British counterparts ended up playing in minor American venues. This 'arrangement' finally collapsed after 1963 when the Beatles and other British rock bands took America by storm.

Many of us would have loved to play music as well as listen to it but the glamorous instruments of the day were clarinets, trumpets (Eddie Calvert was a big star) and drum kits and all of these were expensive. An additional cost was that you really needed to have lessons to learn how to play them. The one instrument that was rarely heard was the guitar for it was seldom a part of the big-band line-up and when it did crop up it was either as the 'novelty' sound of the American duo Les Paul and Mary Ford or the Spanish or Latin America sounds of acts such as 'Dorita y Pepe.' Later, of course, it became the most popular musical instrument of all, aided by Bert Weedon's 'Play in a Day' book. There were also a few American 'country and western' acts and folk or blues artistes such as Burl Ives, Josh White and Big Bill Broonzy. They were allowed to come and perform in Britain, unlike the American bands and instrumentalists who were barred by the Musicians Union, as they were classified as 'variety artistes', not musicians.

However, around 1955 a revolution began which was to change popular music for ever. We were already becoming aware of a new sound from America called 'rock and roll' and knew of its leading stars, especially Bill Haley. At the same time, in Britain, a new and really very simple musical style suddenly became popular. This was called 'skiffle' and it had a real effect on me and thousands of others. It started when the banjo player from the Chris Barber Jazz Band, Lonnie Donegan, had a surprising hit record called Rock Island Line. It was just Lonnie himself on guitar and vocal, with a double bass player and (very strangely) a washboard providing the percussion. I thought this was fantastic and its simple format suddenly made everyone aware that it was possible for me or anyone to make music. All of the early skiffle hits were based upon black American folk songs but would-be musicians soon discovered that there were other avenues they could explore. Thus the early songs of Elvis Presley like Heartbreak Hotel and Hound Dog and those of the other new rock and roll stars such as Tommy Steele (with his cover of Guy Mitchell's Singing the Blues) and Bill Haley and the Comets' Rock Around the Clock could be played by anyone with a guitar and the ability to play just three chords on it. In fact, the guitar was the only 'real' musical instrument needed as the others could be created at home.

I had a friend in the scouts called Johnny ('Fingers') Hammond who was very keen to become a drummer so I bought a washboard and we made a tea chest bass and set about trying to make music. A friend soon had to take over the bass and I bought a guitar. This meant a trip to Westbourne Arcade and the home of Mr Don Strike and his family. In those days (1955) he didn't have the shop (which is still there)

The Ron Westcott Jazzmen c1960 rehearsing in Charminster. L-R Ron Chilcott, Trombone. Ron Westcott, Trumpet. Don Morgan, Clarinet. David Greenway, Piano. Terry McDonald, Guitar. Keith Poppett, Drums.

Ron Westcott Jazzmen again with, Terry on banjo this time, and Alan Harris on bass.

The Biddles - Liz Heaslip, Don Morgan and Terry McDonald. c.1964

but instead you went upstairs to his flat and the guitars were laid out on his bed! They were of course only acoustic, none of your electric stuff then! Don Strike taught guitar and banjo and sold instruments from the flat.

Now my brother Terry had also fallen in love with skiffle and was way ahead of me. He was already an accomplished guitarist and he hated me playing his as he claimed I played it too hard and put it out of tune! He had also bought his first guitar from Mr Strike, paying £5 for it plus another £1 for a case and he paid for it in four weekly instalments of £1.50 from his £3.60 a week wage from Flight Refuelling where he worked.

He went on to play guitar and banjo in a traditional jazz band and then, in the mid 1960s became deeply involved in the folk music revival. He, his friend Don Morgan (who had played clarinet in jazz bands with Terry) and a girl called Liz Heaslip formed a trio called 'The Biddles' (it was Dorset dialect for 'beetles') and were very successful, performing at folk clubs all over southern England and even made a few radio and television appearances. They also won a competition (along with three other English groups) to perform at a major festival in the Republic of Ireland.

With some reluctance Terry showed me the three chords that you needed to play basic rock and roll, namely E, A, and B7, and that was it! I could now play a twelve bar blues! Incidentally Paul McCartney and John Lennon had a similar experience when they started their first group but they

The Biddles - Don, Liz and Terry.

knew only two chords – E and A. However, they had heard that a man who lived the other side of town knew how to play a B7 so they went to seek him out and when he showed them how play it, they too had the three chord trick! We, of course, already had the three chords and had the makings of a group but we still needed a real musician to complete the line up.

A chance meeting one day outside my friend Martin Gibbs' house on the corner of Linden and Livingstone Roads was the big breakthrough. I was introduced to Roy Phillips. He stood there, guitar in hand but at that time did not know any chords - he must have bought it that day. This was my big moment because I knew three, E, A and B7 of course, and Roy was impressed, in fact he was so impressed that he joined our group. But Roy was already a very accomplished piano player and could also read music. He was playing in professional dance bands from when he was about 12 or 13 and there had even been an article in the Poole and Dorset Herald about him. From this meeting, then, came the start of a new life in live music for me.

We practised most nights in John's front room, at his parent's small semi detached house in Salisbury Road. How the neighbours put up with it I'll never know! John soon beat the washboard flat as he played it with drumsticks and not thimbles! So, a proper drum set was needed and it was not too long before John had one but it must have been made around 1930. I can't remember where it came from but it consisted of a large narrow bass drum with coconuts on top, a snare drum, and a small high-hat This was the kit of a strict tempo dance band and we were playing rock roll on it, but it sounded great to us, especially after the flattened washboard!

Our first gig was at Parkstone Darby and Joan Club and we went down well after playing Singing the Blues about four times and Rock Around the Clock about six times. It was followed by a wedding reception in the Co-op hall at the top of Churchill Road and this was a bit more difficult as they all wanted to dance. Luckily Roy could play the piano so we managed to get by. One thing I remember was that it was the first time I heard the record Roll over Beethoven (1956) by Chuck Berry and it blew me away! I also remember playing Upton Labour Club which was a wooden hut at this time and it had a coal burning pot belly stove in the middle of the room. I remember this one because my mum and dad came to it but I don't think they were impressed by our musicianship.

We called our group The Planets and we started to pick up more gigs as we became more confident. John bought a new white Premier drum kit that had everything. He also bought a blue 'Tommy Steele' suit that was on display in the front corner window of the Ashley Road Co-op. The suit was covered with pictures of guitars and he cut quite a dash in it! We entered a talent competition being held at the Moderne cinema in Winton, although this was very difficult for us as you had to sing and play at ten o'clock in the morning. It's not easy when you are an evening band but we did our best although we did not win it. However, it was at this gig that we met someone called Tony Arnold who was a bit strange or so we though. He wore a Stetson hat, was obsessed with country music and had a really stupid nickname ('Brush Atkins') that he insisted on being called.

We went home to his house and he showed us his record collection and soon after he joined our group and played a few gigs with us, but his style of music really did not fit in with our rock and roll style band. He later became famous with his recording studio 'Arnie's Shack' in Bournemouth. Another competition that we entered was at the Royal Ballrooms in Boscombe and there must have been twenty bands playing that night. We did well and didn't come last!

After various friends trying to play with us we settled on Barry Southgate as our new member. Barry came from the Trinidad estate and soon became a part of the band. There were now four of us, three guitars and the drums. The bass guitar had yet to be invented. Our repertoire was typically based around the songs made by popular by American acts such as the Everley Brothers, Buddy Holly, Chuck Berry, Little Richard, Gene Vincent and, of course, Elvis Presley. We also copied British artistes such as Cliff Richard and the Drifters (who later became the Shadows), Billy Fury and Marty Wilde.

One night, in the winter of 1956, we all went to Poole to attend a dance at the Centenary Hall, above Poole Labour Club near the George Roundabout, which was a big dance venue in Poole in those days. We had some beer, danced with the local girls, did the fashionable dance of the time called 'the Creep', but mainly we were impressed with the bands! During one of the breaks we started talking to one of the bands and told them of our small group and of our aspirations to hit the big time! They introduced us to their manager, a 'Mr Big' called Reg Calvert who, it turned out, was looking for new talent. He said that if we could get back to the dance before it finished he would give us a try out. We jumped at this opportunity and dashed home on the bus to collect all of our kit and get back to the dance by half past ten. By some miracle and with the help of Hants and Dorset we just made it for the other bands were packing up as we arrived in the hall. We set up our gear and I think Johnny played someone else's drum kit. We played a couple of numbers and sounded great, even if I say so myself! As a result, we were taken on, on the spot, by the Southampton group impresario Reg Calvert.

Reg Calvert in his radio station at Shivering Sands.

Our first gig under 'professional' management was Branksome Conservative Club which was 'up on hill!' The dance hall was upstairs and we played there every Tuesday night from then on.

The Calvert formula was three groups per night and we did half hour spots in two sessions. On Fridays it was Christchurch British Legion and this was a tough gig for us as we had to travel there by bus! By now our guitars were electric but we didn't need amps as you played through the on stage P.A. System. Reg was clever and made the equipment himself and there was a small square box on the stage floor which had multi jack sockets so you just plugged in and played. We were paid promptly on the night in little brown envelopes. Very efficient was Mr Calvert.

We were getting a lot of work through Reg Calvert, not only playing Branksome

Branksome Conservative Club as it was in the fifties

Conservative Club on Tuesday evenings but the Centenary Hall in Poole on Thursdays. It was at a gig at this latter venue that we became embroiled in a row between Reg Calvert and the local branch of the Musicians' Union. The Centenary Hall was owned and managed by the Labour Party and was therefore opposed to any form of non-union labour working there. The same rules applied to the Woodlands Hall, above Parkstone Labour Club. In November 1958, Eddie Francis, who was a local dance-band leader and secretary of the local Musicians' Union branch tried to stop us playing because he alleged we were not members of the union. He was correct but we claimed that we were actually members of the Southampton Branch. Mr Francis's view prevailed as far as the Centenary Hall was concerned, but we were able to move the Thursday evening dances to the Shaftesbury Hall, Poole. The dispute made the front page of the Poole and Dorset Herald under the headline of 'Union Knocks the Rock – Promoter and Band Leader in Battle.' It was a classic example of the way in which the old world of music did not know what to make of the new, teenage phenomenon of self made rock and roll!

One evening, on the 'Yellow Bus' on our way to our Friday evening gig at Christchurch British Legion, a terrible accident befell me. The only place to put all our gear was upstairs on the rear parcel shelf, so guitars and drums were all piled up together but when we came to get off the bus I found that my guitar was broken in half! I had to borrow one for the gig to get by, but luckily Don Strike was able to put it back together.

A new name for the group was needed so the manager decided that it should be called 'Roy Phillips and the Royal Blue Rockers.' Reg had us kitted out in matching

Union trouble!!

blue silk tops and had a publicity photo shoot.

John's sister was a hair dresser and she dyed hair with peroxide, so John, Roy, and I decided we would look more rock and roll with blond hair! So we went to the local Boots the Chemist in order to purchase a large bottle of peroxide and a tooth brush to apply it with. That Saturday morning, in John's kitchen in Salisbury road we set about becoming blonds! John went for the 'Full Monty' i.e., all over, Roy had a strip down the middle like a badger, and I just did my quiff amid fears that my Mum and Dad would go mad, but they never noticed or if they did they never said anything about it!

As rock 'n' roll musicians we felt we needed to look the part, from hairstyles to footwear! My hair dresser was Phil Scott's on the Ashley road near Albert Road and the style I favoured was a Tony Curtis with a 'D.A.' at the back and plenty of Brylcreem to keep it in shape. Mr Scott had cut our family hair from day one and 'Scotty', as Dad called him, had a small plank that was placed across the arms of the chair to lift you up to be seen to! A good gauge of your maturity was when the plank was no longer offered. Outside his shop was the bus stop for the 'Rossmore Flyer' the bus service provided by a private company run by a Mrs Louie Dingwall who also trained race horses at stables on Sandbanks and raced them along Sandbanks beach.

However, the purchase of a pair of white shoes from the shoe market shop up on hill was a purchase too far for my parents and a very upset rocker was sent back to the shop to exchange them for a pair of sensible proper shoes after Dad had gone mad from the shock of seeing the white ones. The only jeans you could buy were black and had no style at all. Drain pipe trousers and winkle picker shoes were the

Roy Phillips - John Hammond - Paul
McDonald - Barry Southgate

Playing Staines Town Hall

Band picture 1958 - Nice quiff.

gear to be seen in and although there were a few 'Teddy Boys' in Parkstone, they were mostly seen in Bournemouth.

But as I gained more independence with my own money I was able to go to the only shop that sold the right stuff and that was ' Sidney's' in St Mary's Street, Southampton. This shop sold real Levi jeans with the treble stitched seams plus copper rivets in the right places, shirts with button down pin through collars, and the corduroy flat caps with the strap and buckle on the back, as worn by Gene Vincent and the Blue Caps in that fantastic film The Girl Can't Help It . We wore them in the band and I also wore mine at work on the railway. Watching The Girl Can't Help It, I saw Little Richard for the first time and he blew me away so much so that I sang all of his songs in our band!

Roy Phillips father was a skilled painter and carpenter and he made the group a full size double bass - this looked fantastic and was made out of hard board painted white with wood graining all over to make it look like a real double bass.

Wood grain was a real skill for it was applied with brush or scraper and did look fantastic. It's a lost art today.

The trouble was it weighed half a ton and as we had no transport of our own it made life difficult on the buses. We once had a gig at the Masonic Hall in Lymington and my Dad drove us there in his old SS type Jaguar. It was a real struggle to get the bass into the car that night and if my memory serves me it was the last gig the home made bass attended! Roy and his Dad now set about making a solid electric guitar basing its design on the Fender Stratocaster with double cutaways, single coil pick-ups and a Formica top. Don Strike helped out with the frets in the neck and finishing! Now for a home made guitar it played really well and Roy played it for many years. It's the guitar in the picture of the band at Staines Town Hall. Roy is on the left and I wonder if he still has it. Probably not!

More gigs followed as we became more professional and Staines Town Hall was a big night for us (well, it is nearly London) and produced the only picture I have of the band playing at a dance! Then we played Southampton Guildhall where Reg Calvert had all his best groups playing on that night and the abiding memories of that night is the size of the stage. We had never stood that far apart before and there were 1500 people on the dance floor.

Music had become a major part of my life and even when we weren't playing in public, the other band members and I would still be together. Sometimes we would be practising but on other occasions we would meet in such new and 'trendy' places such as the Copa Cabana Coffee Bar in Ashley Cross. We would spend the whole evening drinking lemon tea in glass cups supported by metal holders. Coffee was still a rather exotic drink to us so we avoided it. We would also go and listen to other bands and musicians at places such as the Parkstone Hotel and the Shipwrights Arms where the powerful voiced folk singer Pete Franklin performed regularly. His girl friend would go round the audience with a pint mug for you to put money in and it was always full by the end of evening.

However, I did have a full-time job as a fireman for British Railways which meant working shifts. I was finding it more and more difficult to juggle work and the band and thinking back now I don't know how I fitted it all in! More time was being spent in Reg's flat in Derby Road, Southampton, with Reg's wife Dorothy and William their pet monkey.

One Saturday we all went to the Pier at Southampton in Reg's Austin Princess car to sing at an audition. There were so many of us that we all could not fit into the car, so I had to ride in the boot. Later that day we left to play a gig in Andover at their top dance venue, the village hall, which was a long green corrugated iron shed! It was at this gig that Roy sang a couple of songs which I found strange as up until then I had done all the singing. That night, on the way back to Southampton, we called into an all night café and I remember we made quite a nuisance of ourselves, mooning in the

Reg's wife Dorothy and the monkey.

shop window and thinking it was hilarious, how very rock and roll. Later that night Reg said he knew a spot by the river were we could go swimming and this we duly did, in the dark with not a clue how deep it was, but we had a ball swimming in the nude with the girls and luckily got away with it! I shivered on the long drive back to Reg's house in Southampton.

The next gig of interest was at Bournemouth Town Hall on a Saturday afternoon. This was a test transmission for the new independent television service, Southern Television. We had to go into make up for this and our faces were dusted with a brown powder - we looked like we been in Barbados for a month, but how fantastic it was playing to TV cameras. What I did not know is that I was soon to play my last gig with the band. This was in Millbrook, Southampton and was not really a gig but rehearsing as backing band to Wee Willie Harris, the flamboyant singer-pianist who was a regular performer on television, and I'm afraid this showed up my Achilles heel. I was a singer and not a guitarist and still had only three chords in my repertoire. This meant I could only play in the key of E and to my horror he wanted to sing in A! I just could not play to a high enough standard. So I sadly left the band that day, walking away and never to play with the boys again. I would occasionally see them at the Sydney Hall in Weymouth and the Drill Hall in Holdenhurst Road, Bournemouth but only as a member of the audience.

Roy went on to play with a number of well-known bands including the Dowland Brothers and the Tornadoes. He also worked with the legendary producer Joe Meek and finally formed his own group the Peddlers where he found a great deal of fame and success! He is still alive and well and now lives in New Zealand. Johnny Hammond went on to play with Rock Circus and with Al Curtly - Al is a brilliant pianist and played with all the big names in Bournemouth but as for Barry, well I just don't know!

Our manager Reg Calvert later found fame as Screaming Lord Sutch's manager and together they formed a pirate radio station called Radio Sutch on an offshore anti-aircraft fort in the Thames at Shivering Sands in May 1964. In September Reg bought out Sutch and started his own station called Radio City. Over the next few months the new station built up a loyal audience in south east England and in September 1965 merger talks began with the most famous of the pirate stations, Radio Caroline. However, a dispute about the ownership of a radio transmitter resulted in Reg being shot dead in June 1966 by one of Radio Caroline's directors, Oliver Smedley. He was subsequently acquitted of Reg's murder after claiming that he had acted in self defence during a violent struggle. Whatever the rights or wrongs of the matter, I shall always remember Reg as a true showman, one of the first in the emerging rock 'n' roll business.

Chapter 4

I left school in the summer of 1956, with no qualifications and no real idea of what I wanted to do. At school, just before leaving, we all had to write a letter to a prospective employer seeking work and mine was to Bolson's ship yard in Poole, asking if they had any vacancies for apprentice shipwrights. They replied saying that there were no vacancies but if one came up they would let me know, and I'm still waiting! The trouble was that I never did expect to hear from them as I had no qualifications, so what was to become of me? I had my fledgling music career but that didn't pay very well so I had to think of something else.

A very tidy Bournemouth shed early 1960's

Just across the road from our house in Churchill Road, was Victoria Crescent where the Fitzell family lived. There were four of them, Mrs Fitzell, her daughter Diana, and her sons Stephen and Derek. Her husband had been in the army and was killed in February 1945, just ten weeks before the end of the war, and she brought up the three children on her own. Diana (who was to marry a railway man) and Stephen both went to the grammar schools but when Stephen left school, he went to work on the railway as a locomotive fireman at Bournemouth Central station. There were other railwaymen living nearby. Three doors down from us lived a mainline driver, Mr Bill Woods, and down in Heavenly Bottom lived fireman Phillip Bunce. I never really got to know him that well. I just remember him as a very quiet boy.

Britain still had an enormous railway network at this time, a legacy from the nineteenth century. Although some redundant lines and stations had been closed after the war there were still 21,000 miles of track and 6,000 stations and, on the rare occasions that we went a long journey, we went by train. Terry remembers the epic wartime journey that Mum undertook with us to go and see Dad who was stationed in Westmorland at the time, presumably training Canadian troops to drive tanks at the Warcop ranges. It is a probably a coincidence that he was a Newfoundlander and those he was training were Canadian. Newfoundland was not, at that time, part of Canada and Dad was in the British Army although he proudly wore the word 'Newfoundland' on his shoulders. The journey to Westmorland involved crowded trains and a number of changes and it must have been quite stressful for Mum to travel so far with a four year old and a two year old. On other occasions we would visit her relatives in Portsmouth and this always meant changing trains at Southampton. She always liked to start the journey at Bournemouth West Station or Branksome because they were near to Upper Parkstone. It was just a short (and cheap) bus ride to Bournemouth West and if we used Branksome Station, we would walk.

It was a chance conversation with Derek, the younger of the two Fitzell brothers (and Terry's best friend) that led me to a railway job. Like his brother, Derek was also working on the railway and he mentioned that there were vacancies for cleaners at Bournemouth shed. Now this appealed to me for I had spent some of my youth train spotting at Parkstone station and also was interested in steam locomotives. So I applied for a job and enclosed my testimonial from the

TEL. PARKSTONE. 4235.

15 Cranbrook Rd
Parkstone
Dorset

19. 7. 06.

Dear Sir,
I have much pleasure in giving Paul McDonald a testimonial, he has been with us as a scout for about 2 yrs, and is a Patrol Leader at the present time, he is a very cheerful and good worker, and I have no hesitation in recommending him to you

Yours Truly
Group Scoutmaster
A. G. Godfram
3rd. Parkstone

only person who I knew at the time with any position in the community, my scout master! And then sat back and waited and soon a letter arrived, asking me to go for an interview with Mr Pringle the Shed Master at Bournemouth locomotive shed.

Well the day arrived and I nervously walked into the shed and asked the first person I saw where the Shed Master's office was. I was directed to the lobby where, through a small hatch, I could see a man who turned out to be the time clerk. I explained why I was there and he told me to go round to the general office. I went to a green door on the side of the shed and knocked nervously. I stepped in and on to

A fantastic picture by Nike Esau, inside Bournemouth shed, years of oil and grease on the shed floor. the driver on the left is reading the notice board.

the polished lino floor which smelt of paraffin. A tall thin man in a suit was sitting behind a desk and I stood before him and answered his questions. I was still only fourteen years old and would not be fifteen until the First of August. I was required to have a full medical as a condition of employment and was issued with a free ticket to travel to British Railways Southern Region headquarters at Eastleigh. On the train that day, also going for a medical, I met a boy called Bill Robinson who lived in New Milton. We were to start work together but he would be senior to me.

On arrival at Eastleigh we had a short walk over the bridge and we found the medical centre, a green timber painted building. The medical consisted of blood pressure, eyesight, colour vision tests, with the new and very strange looking 'ishirara' cards , and then the worst bit the rupture test, this consisted of dropping your trouser and underpants while the doctor grasped your testicles and said 'cough!' I passed the medical so the job was mine and after reporting back to Bournemouth shed the next question was "When can you start?" I said the second week in September as I had booked my last holiday with the scouts in August. We were going to Beer in Devon for summer camp and I did not want to miss it. Unbeknown to me at the time I had just made a serious mistake in not starting as soon as possible because seniority was every thing on the railway and this was to have a serious effect on my later career.

The big day dawned and at 8.00 AM, sharp, I presented myself to the cleaner foreman Mr Tom Glassey. Tom was a small man, about 5ft, I think, but was well respected by us boys. My first job was a trip to the stores to be kitted out with a grease-top hat and a new set of blue overalls. Two sets were issued, wrapped in brown paper and tied with string and after rolling up the trouser legs (which were too long) I was ready for work. I was issued with a bundle of clothes and a bucket of paraffin and oil mix and told 'follow me son' and off we went into the cavernous confines of Bournemouth loco shed.

Tom showed me how to fold the cloth properly to get the best out of each one. The cloth was folded to give eight faces, and Tom checked that each cloth was used properly. If you were issued with ten cloths then Tom had to have ten back or you were in trouble. The cloths used were 'thirds' or in other words, had already been washed twice. When the cloths were new they were white and fluffy and issued very sparingly, one for one from the stores, as face cloths and only to be used with railway regulation soap. A side affect was that on the more mature members of staff white fluff stuck to the stubble on their chins. This amused us boys! When cloths were returned to the stores as seconds they were issued more freely for general use, i.e. on the footplate holding hot fire irons or used by the driver when oiling up a loco for traffic. By the third wash they were only fit for loco cleaning. All of them were sent to Eastleigh works for washing where all the oil was extracted from the dirty cloths and recycled as lamp oil! Very Victorian but super efficient! Tom showed me how to clean the paint work properly, dipping a cloth in the oil and paraffin mix, wring it out and apply to the filthy loco, rub in a circular motion on an area two foot square and then polish with a clean cloth. Move along and do the same again.

I quickly made new friends including Alan Mabey who started the same day as me, John Creech, Bill 'Robbo' Robinson, John Wyatt, Ian McNulty Barry Whitmarsh, 'Konky' Phelps, John Boyt who had a very bad stutter, John Dimmock, tall and very thin, and Ray Rowse who had access to a horse on Turbary Common which on one wild afternoon we rode bare back. Like several of the other cleaners he had a motor cycle, a BSA Bantam, on which us boys bombed up and down the back road at dinner time and tried to ride up the steep bank behind the cycle shed. There was also Chris Tabor (who later had a Norton Dominator), Frank Farwell and Henry Rawles. Henry lived in Wool and was allowed to come into work late. He would come in on the up Royal Wessex getting in to Bournemouth Central Station at 8.30. One other was Andrew Gates who lived in Winston Avenue, Branksome, and who had an old black car in a lockup garage which he polished as he waited to pass his driving test!

As well as cleaning duty there were other jobs such as 'bum boy' which was nowhere near as bad as it sounds for it simply involved carrying letters and messages to and from the station master to the loco shed office. You also had to run errands for all the shed staff such as fetching cigarettes, pipe tobacco, fish and chips, and tins of Carnation condensed milk for the boiler wash-out staff who, by the way, drank the strongest tea you ever saw in your life!

If you were lucky, there was 'notifying' in the afternoon. The notes were issued

Two standard tanks, Class 4 & 3, stand at the bottom of the shed under the smoke chutes.

from the Roster Clerk and were for late change of duty and this was seen as a good 'skive' for once all your notes were delivered you could go home! The only problem that could arise was when you knocked on the door and no one answered, as you had to hand the note to the driver or fireman in person, or take the note back to the shed.

I enjoyed notifying for I would take my push bike on the train to the nearest station and ride out into the country trying to find the location down some back lane. After a time you got to know where most members of staff lived and nearly always got home early. Another job was chopping firewood for the steam raiser to light up dead locos. Two cleaners would be assigned this work, down the bottom of Number 1 Road, where a five plank wooden wagon sat, full of old sleepers. These were lifted out of the wagon, laid across the saw horses, and then with a huge cross-cut saw, sawn into thirds, split with an axe and piled up in a corner. This was hard work for a fifteen year old, on the cross-cut saw and axe all day long.

During the winter, senior cleaners would return to cleaning duties, when there was no firing work out on the road. These lads were not just senior to us but in the

Although not Bournemouth shed it brings it home for me just how young we were
(picture by W. Philip Conolly)

pecking order were far superior to us, and in fact did no cleaning work at all, except chase us younger lads around. Cleaners worked in pairs on small tank engines and four were required to clean a tender loco. As you became more experienced you always left a small dirty patch to clean latter on the corner of the tender so it looked like you were still working. As you always had some work left to do then it was off to the bowels of the shed for fun and games such as running through the pits under the locos or climbing up into the smoke chutes over the top of the engines. Water fights with buckets were common and, at the very worst if you were caught, you'd get a soaking from the water hydrants down the middle of the four roads in the shed. Leather riveted hoses with brass nozzles were connected to the hydrants and if somebody turned one of these on you the jet of water would knock you over. You would then spend the rest of the afternoon drying out by the sand furnace. Setting fire to other cleaners' pockets was common and a smouldering cloth in your pocket would go un noticed for sometime by then it was to late and your pocket was full of holes just like everyone else's.

Card schools in the firebox of a dead loco were common too. An upturned bucket with a head code disc on top served as a table and lit by a flare lamp up on the brick arch, a card school would take place. Now Tom Glassy had spent decades chasing young oily cleaners around the shed and knew all their tricks and he always found you with his cry 'come on, let's have yer!' If you saw him coming, you'd make a quick dash back to the loco to your four-foot square dirty patch an act like you'd never left it. Another trick that the cleaners enjoyed playing took place during the winter. The shed would be lined with braziers burning by the hydrants and under the water columns and it was the cleaners' job to keep them going. Somebody would urinate into an old baked bean tin, put it on the brazier, rapidly depart, and a few minutes later as it boiled over you would hear the hollers and shouts of anguish from the shed fitting staff at the unbelievably pungent smell. The guilty individual had, of course, long-since fled!

The cleaning day was from 8 till 5, five days a week. We also had a night shift which was 12.01 AM until 8.01 and you were brought in on this shift to clean the 'down' newspaper train and the 'up' Wessex loco. This took approximately two hours and as there was no cleaner foreman on duty, only the loco running foreman who had enough on his plate worrying about loco crews to bother about us, so it was easy to lose yourself. We spent most of the rest of the shift asleep, lying on the tables and benches in the cleaners' cabin. These were rock hard but I learnt at a very early age to sleep anywhere.

Getting to Bournemouth from Parkstone was not easy, and for that first year, I rode my bicycle, either all the way, down through Bourne Bottom, along Surrey Road, up into Glenferness Avenue, in to East Avenue, down to Cemetery Junction then left into Beechey Road, through the gate, down the ramp and into the loco shed. A simpler and more attractive alternative was to ride to Branksome Station where, if lucky, I would hop on a train.

Tom Glassey & Jack Whyte a fitter, stand together on number I road in front of Merchant Navy 35018 British India Line. it looks as if the loco is being prepared for work (note the oil can on the side framing).

Coaling down at Salisbury was a tough job. Here two men help the fireman of this 'up' Waterloo Express to shovel forward the dust that's left for the last 84 miles. Good luck!!!

Once I reached my sixteenth birthday, my life changed in two ways. Firstly, I was now available to be trained as a fireman, and secondly, I was old enough to get a provisional driving licence so I bought a moped from Taylor's bicycle shop on the corner of Davis Road in Tennyson Buildings, Ashley Road. It was a Paloma and its registration number was MTK 557. I loved this bike. I suddenly had the independence to go where I wanted, and go I did at full throttle, rather like Toad of Toad Hall in The Wind in the Willows! It certainly made getting to work so much easier.

It was during the summer of 1957 that I and my friend Alan Mabey decided to go on holiday to a Butlin's Holiday Camp and we chose Pwllheli in North Wales because, with our free rail tickets we could travel anywhere in the country, so Pwllheli it was! I remember the train journey well. We caught our train from Bournemouth West station to Waterloo. We then went by tube to King's Cross where we changed at Crewe for Conway and Pwllheli. We made friends with a group of lads from Wallasey near Liverpool. I dated a waitress and we met when she finished work at nine o'clock and we walked down to the beach for a kiss and a cuddle. I also entered a talent competition and sang a Little Richard song, coming second and won a set of clothes brushes! Most useful. The picture below shows me with Alan in the dining room at Butlins.

Back at work, the first duties for a trainee fireman were coaling down. At Branksome shed we would go to the stores and be issued with a number 8 shovel. Then we'd walk over to the Central Station down platform and meet the Bournemouth Belle as it arrived, with its Nine Elms cockney crew on board. We would ride with them round to Bournemouth West and then propel the stock up through

MODEL TTA

Ideal economy moped driven with the simplicity of a cycle. 2 controls only—twist grip throttle control, handlebar lever brakes.
Multimatic clutch which engages automatically when required.

Lavalette motor.

49.7 c.c. 2 stroke,
technical detail (see back page).
Fully adjustable riding position.
Handlebars and wheel rims heavily chromium plated.
Tyres 23 x 200 white-wall (Dunlop).
Petrol tank capacity 1¼ gallons.
Finish—Beige or Mercedes Blue.

Price : £54 19s. 11d.

(Including Purchase Tax)

If you can ride a cycle

Paloma brochure

Alan Mabey and I at Butlin's Holiday Camp, Pwllheli.

Rear view of Branksome shed. The little hut on this end is the drivers' cabin; a good place to brew tea and enjoy some railway banter.

the carriage-washer, taking care to close the cab windows or else get very wet! We'd leave the stock in the sidings, for servicing, and then run light-engine around the Branksome Triangle to turn and then in to Branksome shed, where the work really started. As the fireman prepared his fire for the return trip and the driver walked round the loco, checking bearings and oiling where necessary, I climbed up into the tender, being careful not to fall down into the huge hole where the fireman had shifted two tons of coal since leaving Waterloo. The remaining coal was at the back of the tender and this had to be shovelled forward. The hardest parts was getting a start, digging down into the coal and trying to find the

Alan Mabey and I in Bournemouth gardens by the pavilion.

sloping metal bed below. Once found, the process was then straightforward, but every now and then you'd hit a rivet and it would jar up through the shovel into your arms. Sometimes the fireman would come up and help you, but mostly not. As soon as they could they were over the fence and on their way to the Woodman pub for a few pints of beer!

I loved working at Branksome shed as it seemed so homely - warm and welcoming. On Bank Holiday weekends in the summer you could be sent to Branksome all day, such was the demand for hand coaling. The steam raiser, who was called Jock, ran a very tight ship and it showed in the tidy state of the shed and yard. In the cabin there was always a kettle on the boil for loco crews to make a brew, but there again this was the old 'Somerset and Dorset' at its best! I heartily disliked those Midland Region locos, with their small gauge frames, complicated fire-hole doors, multi level floors – they were just not at all like our superb Southern locos.

Once back at Bournemouth shed it was a trip out as 'third man.' This meant riding as a passenger on the footplate, watching and learning and, if lucky, given a go on the shovel. Now the shovel is quite an inanimate object, but in the hands of an experienced fireman it could come to life. Looking through his eye lashes and seeking for thin spots in the fire, he could place coal exactly where needed over a 5ft wide by 9ft long fire box. Enormous skill was needed to do this as all the time the fireman was riding the bucking bronco that was the loco footplate at high speed. He had to fire little and often, keeping the steam pressure gauge near to the red line, as well as maintaining boiler water levels and looking out for all signals on his side. He had also to keep the footplate clean and well washed down with the 'pep' pipe.

The Woodman pub, Branksome.

We also attended classes in the 'Mutual Improvement Cabin' which was really a grounded vintage carriage body, down the back road and opposite the 75ft turntable. Inside were diagrams of loco parts such as Wallshart's valve gear, Stephenson's valve gear, the Bulleid valve gear, plus the vacuum ejectors and water injectors. The names of all the parts had to be learned. Last but not least, there was the hardest part of all and this was the Rule Book and the most important was Rule 55 which covered the protection of the train when stopped at fixed signals. If you were standing at a signal that showed 'danger' for more than five minutes (you would have blown the whistle to alert the signalman of your presence) and there was no movement from the signal, you would carry out Rule 55 which entailed going to the signal box in person and signing his register. The procedure was 'line, time, sign' and very often you found that the last thing the signalman wanted was an oily, dirty, greasy fireman walking into his polished workplace so he would usually be standing at the door, holding the train register saying 'sign here, son – I'll get you away as soon as I can.'

Loco inspector Jack Evans at Waterloo.

I was to pass out as a fireman on a Charley class C1, 0-6-0, whilst working a goods train around the old road, and firing up Wimborne bank under the watchful gaze of loco inspector Jack Evans. Standing proud in his trilby hat and black rubber mac, he duly pronounced me fit to be a fireman.

So that was it - express trains here I come! Yes, for sure, but how long would I have to wait? After all, at Bournemouth shed in the fifties, it was dead man's shoes.

I was given a few turns on the Bournemouth yard shunter, moving wagons around and shunting them into their correct formation to make up the train. I was working on the old Adams tank loco and this was the start of climbing a very long ladder. These turns involved being at Bournemouth Central goods yard, shunting all night on a small tank engine with a driver near to retirement who had nothing in common with a 16 year old rocker! So conversation was, to say the least, minimal. But looking after the boiler all night kept you busy enough and you had to keep an eye out for the 'shunter.' This was the man on the ground coupling and un-coupling the rakes of wagons and calling out 'hit em up' to go forward or 'whoa' to stop. At night all shunting was done by paraffin lamp. In bad weather such as in fog or falling snow the audible whistle code was used - one for go ahead, two was set back, three stop, and four was to ease up.

Working on Bournemouth Central station shunter was a very boring turn for you had to sit outside the loco shed in the long head shunt on the up side, waiting for the Waterloo trains to arrive from Bournemouth West station and then adding the Weymouth section, to make up the full length train of some twelve cars! For the long trip to London plus trips up to Bournemouth goods yard to pick up wagons of loco coal. There was also a Bournemouth West station shunter and Poole goods yard

Loco-men Pope, Robinson and Walters sharing a can of tea and a game of cards in Nine-Elms Drivers' cabin (Photo Courtesy Jim Robinson collection)

shunter. The Poole duty was alright as there was banking of certain trains up Parkstone bank, and on a Tuesday night you could climb up the goods yard water tower and watch the Poole Pirates speedway match.

After gaining experience as a fireman on shunting turns, the next step-up was with the Poole bug gang, working the little B4 0.4.0 shunting engine. There were two turns in this gang, early or late, and on the early turn you had to get the loco ready. The fire box was very small but we still managed to put an enormous amount of coal in it! We then had to fill the side bunkers up and also pile as much coal as you could on the all ready cramped footplate as it had to last all day. We would then set off 'light engine' for the trip to Poole. This was quite a slow journey as the bug did not like to go too fast and there were also some drivers who knew the windows to look in as ladies were getting dressed They especially liked coasting past the rear of Florence Road, in Lower Parkstone, as some people there never pulled their curtains. I think

The bug on a long freight train.

the people in the houses felt safe looking out over a dark railway line but how wrong they were!

The run down Parkstone bank was interesting as all the braking was down to the fireman and on one memorable trip it all went wrong for one fireman, 'Konky' Phelps. As the little loco neared Branksome the steam pressure was slowly falling until there was not enough steam to move forwards. The driver was not too pleased with this situation and demanded that Konky stir the fire up and generate more steam. Konky opened the fire-hole door and was shocked when he realised what was wrong. The fire had gone out! This meant a walk to the nearest signal box and request a tow

Running around its train on a busy day on the Quay.

back to Bournemouth shed. What had gone wrong? Konky had simply put too much coal on and had blacked the fire out!

Upon arrival at Poole station we would shunt into the siding next to the down road platform, which had a gate at the end leading to the tram way to the Quay. After picking up the few vans and coal wagons that usually made up our train, the shunter would open the gates and out onto the streets we would trundle - around Nile Row, past Market Street and then down West Quay Road with the shunter walking in front with his red flag. Now this was never easy because of the parked cars left on the track. Usually a blow on the whistle was enough but sometimes it was all hands to bump the offending cars clear! On past BDH and you knew you were there because of the most appalling smell that came from this drug factory. We soon left the smell behind and around the corner was the Quay side where there would be empty coal wagons waiting to change over for our full ones. Sometimes you might see the men loading coal onto the paddle steamers by hand with wicker baskets and the steamers I remember are the Monarch , the Embassy and the Matapan. This last vessel had been a war-time motor torpedo boat. Harvey's and Davis's were the two rival boat companies that operated from the Quay. Harvey's boats were yellow and Davis's were blue.

The Quay was a very busy working dock in those days with coal boats being unloaded under the large gas works transporters. There was grain for Christopher Hill and timber for Sydenham's. The Quay was an interesting place to spend an hour whilst shunting the wagons that we had brought down and then making up the train of empties to return to the station. On a sunny day there was no better place to be and if lucky you might get a smile from a pretty girl!

Coal boat under the transporter.

Hamworthy goods.

A group of young men enjoying themselves on the sorry-looking flying boats lay on the beach. The story goes that they were dragged up on to the beach by Joey Harman with a block and tackle chained to the railway track, prior to being cut up for scrap.

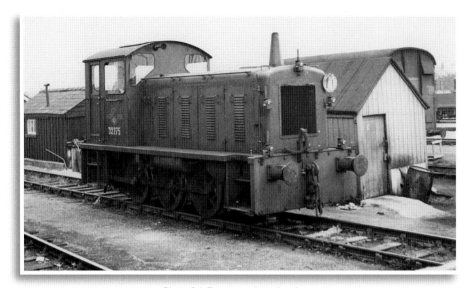
Class 04 Drewry shunting loco.

After the trip down to the quay, we worked a goods train to Hamworthy Junction and picked up any freight to go down the branch to Hamworthy goods or on to New Quay. On this track you could see the Sunderland flying boats lying up on the beach, waiting to be dismantled for scrap. Other sights included people fishing from the nearby power station outfall and boat loads of apples waiting to be loaded into dirty coal wagons for making cider.

At the end of our shift we were relieved by the late turn crew who had walked to us from Poole station. My driver, Wilf Selby, would have his push bike on top of the loco boiler where it had been all day as for him it was just a short ride home. For me it was a walk back to Poole Station in order to catch the first train to Branksome and home without going back to Bournemouth shed.

In the 1950s the railway had probably the largest unsupervised work force in the country, most of its employees being left without management all day. The driver knew the duty and just got on with it! There was no clocking in or out, you simply told the list clerk, Fred Scott, you were there. The driver filled out his daily ticket and when as with Wilf Selby, he would ask the late turn driver to put it in for him at Bournemouth. There were, though, signs of change beginning to appear within the railway industry. In June 1960, for example, I found myself working as second man on the new diesel locos that were replacing the B4 steam locos on the Hamworthy branch line. The new class 04 Drewry loco was a world away from the old 'bug' for it was clean , did not have a fire to look after, and you just had to park it, turn it off and go home!

My next job was a 'promotion' to the 'Sh*t and Shovel' or 'Old Man's Gang.' This was made up of drivers who for various reasons were unable to drive on the main line and newly qualified drivers straight from firing on the main line and then passed for driving. These new drivers moved down to the Old Man's Gang at the bottom of the very long ladder to work their way up to one day drive on the mainline again. For me this was real progress at last because we actually went somewhere!

Q Class 30539 leaving Swanage goods yard with an up freight in September 1961.

Alan Mabey and I outside our Butlins chalet.

Destinations included Ringwood via the old road, Hamworthy via Upton, Broadstone and Swanage with a pickup goods train. Usually the loco would be a Q class 30541 (which survives to this day at the Bluebell Railway in Sussex) and we would shunt the clay sidings at Furzebrook on the way back to Wareham. But mainly the work was preparing locos on the early shifts and disposing on late turn.

My life at this time was very hectic as playing in the band and working shifts did not go together that well. The only time I could go out in the evening was when I was on an early shift and sometimes 'early' was 2.45 am. I would go to bed at midnight and rely on my Mum to get me up at 2.00 o'clock to be on duty at 2.45! This, although exhausting, did generally work but on the odd occasion I would fall asleep down stairs and be found by Mum who promptly sent me on to work, better late than never, and to face the wrath of the running foreman.

In the autumn of 1958 I was 'roistered' in red as a permanent fireman with my own permanent mate, driver Charlie Loveless. Charlie was an old man and very near to the end of his railway career and was restricted to working in the shed and not allowed to go out on the main line. This was it then. Through my lack of seniority I had ended up in the turning gang. There would be no more dashing about on the main line for the foreseeable future, just walking around the shed for eight hours a day with an old man! We worked two shifts, late afternoon and nights, sorting out the locos for the next day's work. As simple as this may seem, Charlie made an art form out of making it difficult. Locos would arrive on shed at the end of their duty and after the disposal crew had finished their work, the loco was left on the pit road and this is where Charlie and I came in.

We would first make sure that the loco had been coaled properly and then we would drive onto the 75 ft turntable, stopping just right in balance in order to assist in turning, wind the reverser into mid gear, screw down the hand brake as hard as you could, then jump down and connect up the long vacuum hogger pipe to the loco whilst your mate blew up the main vacuum jet. This started the motor on the turn table and you then pulled the locking bolt out, put her in gear and away you went! Now this was where the grubby bit of paper in Charlie's pocket came in as of course you need to know what this loco is doing tomorrow, what time is it off-shed, which way round does it need to be - up to London or down to Weymouth? All of this dictated where you berthed the loco. Can you position it now or do you put it in the back road to be moved later? Try as hard as you could to sort it out, as early in the evening as you could, the one loco that you needed to go in behind all the others would not arrive on shed until midnight! On the plus side, though, Charlie let me

34004 rebuilt west country 'Yeovil' on Bournemouth turntable, with Malcom Collop in charge. (photo by Mike Esau)

Parkstone station on a lovely sunny afternoon. a local train is arriving on the down platform, whilst in the goods yard 0-4-0 Pecket saddle tank, 'George Jennings' has just come up the branch from Jennings' Potteries.

drive. Now this was strictly against the rules but management turned a blind eye to this, mainly because it was almost impossible for Charlie to do the job without my help. I was young, fit and agile and could nip in and out, coupling and uncoupling and he was just the opposite.

However, in the summer of 1959 I was back on the footplate and could say 'good bye turning gang!' I was now a 'proper' fireman again travelling on mainline trains, sometimes as far as Waterloo, or down to Weymouth and up to Salisbury. But whilst I was working the early morning school train around the 'old road' (Broadstone to Brockenhurst) in October 1959, I made a very big mistake indeed. We were going along nicely on a 76 Standard but coal dust from the tender started to come into the foot plate. Without looking I reached under my seat for the tender spray valve but opened the 'pep pipe' (the hose pipe fed from the live steam injector for washing down the footplate) by mistake, with the near fatal result that boiling water shot out of it and like a snake the pipe whipped around the footplate, spraying my right leg and face, but mainly in my left eye! Luckily the driver quickly got the situation under control by stamping on the pipe, and I turned it off, I covered my face with a cold wet rag and slumped on to my seat in shock and despair fearing the worst. Would I lose the sight of my left eye? We were, of course, running at line speed at the time 60 mph but this meant that I was now just a passenger and it was all down to the driver to do his job and mine as well! A message was given to the signalman at Holmsley for assistance at Brockenhurst and that is how it transpired.

An ambulance was standing on the platform when we reached Brockenhurst and I was taken first to Lymington hospital, and then transferred to Southampton Eye Hospital where I stayed for a week. Strangely, all that I can remember about that stage of the incident is worrying about my oily boots on the blankets of the stretcher.

Upon returning home I was booked off sick for six weeks and attended Westbourne Eye Hospital as an outpatient. After an eye test with the railway doctor at Eastleigh I was pronounced fit and returned to work in the turning gang! Oh, no - not the turning gang again!

I stayed with the railway for another year, enjoying my work as a fireman on the footplate but, unfortunately, in the autumn of 1960 a new winter roster was published, I found myself put back into the turning gang. I just could not face another winter of walking around Bournemouth Central Loco Shed. With hindsight, writing fifty years later, I realise that with my seniority, I could have applied for (and would have been accepted) a main-line firing position at Nine Elms in London. At the time, though, this never occurred to me although dozens of other railwaymen did just that.

I left the railway in October 1960 and started work at Sykes Potteries in Creekmoor, working on the sand and lime brick plant and shovelling sand in to a hopper all day. This really was boring, but it was day work and my weekends were now my own. The plant I worked on was very old and was always breaking down. The sand that I shovelled was fed into a mixing chamber where it meet the lime which came in large paper bags and Syd the lime man had the job of cutting open the bags and pouring the contents into the hopper. He wore old sacks over his head to protect him from the lime but to no avail for he was covered in the white stuff from head to foot, and his lips were green as he wore no face mask. The lime was delivered in a Ford Thames Trader tipper lorry from Shillingstone Lime Company. We all helped to unload it and stack it in the lime shed. Then water was added to the mix and then, under compression, the brick was forced up on to the large round table through a die. As the table rotated, the brick popped up and had to be gently picked up and placed on the little flat-bed wagon that stood on the rails which led to the auto-clave. Too much pressure and the brick would crumble in your hands.

FIREMAN SCALDED ON FOOTPLATE

Parkstone youth in eye hospital

PAUL McDONALD, an 18-year-old British Railways fireman, was badly scalded while riding on the footplate of a train between Ringwood and Brockenhurst yesterday and was rushed from Brockenhurst to Lymington Hospital by ambulance.

Mr. McDonald, of 87, Churchill-road, Parkstone, had severe injuries to his face, right leg and left eye and was transferred to Southampton Eye Hospital.

His mother was contacted by British Railways officials and taken to Southampton where she was met by a Southern Region welfare officer who took her by car to the hospital.

Mr. McDonald's condition today was said to be "fairly comfortable."

Cutting from 'Echo'

71

The new bricks were built up in a pyramid shape and trolley after trolley was filled throughout the day. Then, with a steel cable drawn down the track to a turn table, one by one they were pushed into the auto clave, a large torpedo shaped tube with a huge door on one end only. When it was full and the door shut and all 30 bolts flogged up with a large spanner and hammer, its contents were then steamed at high pressure over night to cook them into hard white sand and lime bricks.

Sykes was a tough place to work and took some sticking to. People would start work at 7am on Monday and be gone by 10 o'clock, never to be seen again, but it was in the gully shop that the really dirty work was done, but strangely, this job was a closed occupation unless you were a Gosling. This family ran the gully shop, a place where the work involved pouring boiling black pitch into the end of the telephone conduit pipes to make a water tight joint for post office cables. These were manufactured in single, double, four way or six way sections and the men doing this work were covered in pitch. When they took off their clothes they stood up on their own. No one knew how much they earned for this hard and uncomfortable work - it was a family secret!

Bluebird Sabrina on display at a country fair.

I left Sykes Pottery in July 1961 and went to work at Bluebird Caravans on Ringwood Road. Dad worked in Sun Regent mill, within the Bluebird factory, on a saw bench where Harold Cribb [M61]was the mill foreman. Dad was instrumental in getting me the job and I worked as a labour in the mill but did not improve my position there. Bluebird was a big employer in the fifties and early sixties, paying over the rate for good tradesmen. The company was owned by Bill Knott who later sold Bluebirds and started B K Caravans in Manning's Heath Road. Dad worked there as well.

Among the men I worked with was Dave Guppy, who worked on the chassis lines as an engineer making brake gear and chassis parts and also fitting jockey wheels.

The finished vans were moved around the site with great skill by a number of drivers in their short-wheelbase Land Rovers. Among the drivers that I remember are Norman Rodgers & Charlie Beck whilst the vans that I remember were the ultra modern Pacific with its veranda at one end, and the little Wren touring van. A lot of the vans made by Bluebird were dispatched by rail from Poole goods yard to be sold at sites all over the country.

I stuck it out at Bluebirds until June 1962 but, with no chance of promotion, I returned to Sykes as a brick setter, setting bricks in the round beehive coal fired kilns. This job was piece work and if you worked really hard you could earn a good wage but you had to run with your wheel barrow all day to achieve this! Drawing the kiln (i.e. taking the bricks out and stacking them up in long rows in the yard) was also very hard work to avoid the heat. The kiln was still very hot making your hair stand on end and you tried to keep as low as possible to avoid the heat. You were of course forced in to this situation because the longer you stood around on day work waiting for the kiln to cool down you weren't earning any money.

Talking of money, horse racing was the obsession of most of the workforce and luckily for them 'Sailor' the kiln burner was a 'bookies' runner'. He came around every day to take the bets. He wore a special leather pouch around his waist where all the betting slips and money was put. The pouch had a time lock on it and as long as it was locked before the first race, the bookmaker honoured all bets. This was, of course, highly illegal in those days but a blind eye was turned by management! My mate on the brick setting had a small radio for the racing results, but on the news that day in October 1962 they reported the possible chance of war with Russia over the Cuban missile crisis. This was a big worry at the time. In the same month, however, I heard a song called Love Me Do by the new group, the Beatles, one lunch time in the new works canteen. I loved it!

In November I left Sykes and started working at Hamworthy Engineering as a radial driller in the hydraulics divisions at Fleets Bridge. In those days the company also had a site on New Quay, next to the Shipwrights' Arms pub, for the pumps and compressor division. At Fleets Bridge everything was under one roof. George Honeybun was the foreman and Mr Parrot, a large stout man who wore a three piece suit, was the works manager. Geordie Coverdale was my setter and was a top man on the job. I learnt a lot from Geordie and one of the skills that he taught me has stayed with me all my life. This was how to sharpen a drill by hand! My best friend and

The Old Shipwrights' Arms pub. I have had many a good night in this pub. You could catch a small rowing boat ferry over the harbour for a modest sum.

mentor was our line inspector Ron Joyce. Ron taught me to understand basic maths and how to read drawings, micrometers, and the more complicated Vernier gauges. You had to have good eye sight to read a Vernier

The winter of 1963 was the worst on record since 1947 and the snow stayed for weeks, making my ride down Old Wareham Road treacherous to say the least. I managed to make it to work every day and was never late. 'Konky' Phelps, who was a former British Rail fireman, worked on a boring machine in the pump section and it was good to see him again. Although not on piece work, all our jobs had a time on them, and you were expected to make time on all jobs. If you couldn't then you were entitled to ask for a re-time and the Time and Motion Department would send down a man in a white coat with a clip board and stopwatch. Usually this was Mr Lake and he just happened to be the father of Greg Lake, who would later become famous as a member of the rock band Emerson, Lake and Palmer. Mr Lake lived in a prefab in Dale Valley Road. He rarely talked about his son, though.

You would try all kind of tricks to get a bit more time on a job, like slower speeds or feeds and taking more time to change tools and load the component to the jig but it rarely worked. The floor was covered with saw dust to soak up the oil which was everywhere and it made your boots curl up at the toes. The clock room was in the open, close by where you clocked in, and after hanging up your coat and bag it was hoisted up in to the roof so if you needed anything you just had to wait till break time!

We worked a 45 hour week, two weeks of days and two weeks of nights. When I was on nights, I would connect up a 'Dansette' record player to the tannoy system and play all the latest records. My work mates would bring in their own LPs and we would all sing along to the rock and roll songs all night while working our drilling machines.

I stayed with Hamworthy Engineering for the next twenty years, moving from semi-skilled machinist to setter and finally, shift foreman in the company's new transmissions division. With hindsight, I was fortunate to be able to move from job to job so easily and to be able to find what could have been, if I so wished, a job for life. Work was so easy to find that it was common for men to leave one job on a Friday and start a new one the following Monday simply because the new employer was paying threepence or sixpence an hour more.

An aircraft factory during the war and, just like Hamworthy, coats and belongings are hoisted up in to the factory roof.

Alan Mabey with his 250 Ambassador Twin.

Alan Mabey (left) and Ian Campbell on the far right at a dance for Longfleet St Mary's Football Club.

Chapter 5

THE MOTORBIKE YEARS 1957-1963

To this day I still love motorbikes and in 2009 I even re-built my 1960 Matchless trials bike. This love of motor cycles probably came from my Dad who, when he was young, had a Vincent which, at the time, was the ultimate British motor bike. But for me it all started with the need to get to work on the railway and having your own transport was an absolute necessity because of the early or late shifts, so I bought a moped! Cars, at this time, were beyond the reach of most young people (and many older ones) and motor bikes (often with a side car for family men) were an affordable form of transport. At work a friendship soon developed with two colleagues, Alan Mabey and Barry Whitmarsh who were both motor cyclists. Barry was older than Alan and me and was already a fireman and he rode a 250 Francis-Barnet Cruiser - very fast! I started to ride pillion with him as I was only 16 as I did not yet have a proper bike of my own. He lived on Sandbanks Road, next to the railway bridge and was fanatical about cleaning his 'Fanny-Barnet.' The engine and carburettor shone with an unbelievable glow - lots of Sovalautosol and newspaper was his secret. Another new friend was Ian Campbell (who for some reason we always called 'Fred') who rode a 250 BSA and lived in Old Farm Road in Oakdale, next to the prefab estate on Dale Valley Road. He was an apprentice electrician with Meggitt Engineering. I, of course, only had my Paloma moped which meant I was simply not in the same league as my older friends with their real motorbikes.

Ian's dad worked at the Royal Ordnance factory in Sopers Lane and their house came with the job. These houses had flat roofs and small windows and were built to be bomb-proof. Alan Mabey rode a 250 Ambassador Twin which was a very smart looking machine with full rear enclosure and resplendent in post office red! Alan lived in Heath Avenue in Oakdale and his father worked at the gas works as a blacksmith. He was a very big and strong looking man and wore a big leather belt and his braces over the outside of his vest.

The roads in the fifties were empty compared to today and of course the compulsory wearing of crash helmets was still fifteen years away (it became the law in June 1973). I used to ride pillion behind Barry Whitmarsh who was the fastest rider in our gang. Barry just rode the road as it unravelled before him, never slowing down for bends and this was extremely exciting and meant that I had to hang on for dear life. But as the months went by I became quite adept at riding pillion. One incident that I remember is the time that one of our number, Bev Jacobs, who rode a Tiger Cub broke down near to Wareham golf course. It was 11pm and we could not leave him there so, sitting on the back of Barry's bike, I held on to Bev's right hand and we towed him along. This worked out really well and good progress was made, but as we approached the twin railway bridges on Blandford Road the police stopped us. The policeman was not very happy with our solution to the broken down motor bike and charged all three of us with dangerous riding. I came off the worse for I received a £10.00 fine and an endorsement for aiding and abetting Barry and £10.00 and another endorsement for adding an abetting Bev! Now £10.00 was a lot of money in the fifties, nearly two weeks' wages! I think Dad helped out lending me some money to pay the fine. To this day I have never understood why I admitted to the policeman that I had a provisional licence as Barry had a full licence and therefore his pillion passengers did not need any licence at all. Unfortunately I think that this one minor incident set my attitude to the traffic police from then on!

One of my friends, Alan Mabey, was due to take his driving test in Dorchester but a few days earlier he had unfortunately crashed on the Ulwell bends just outside Swanage. These are, sadly, no longer there as the road was straightened in the Sixties. In order to take his test, Alan borrowed Barry's 'Fanny Barnet' but on the way to Dorchester they crashed on a bend in Puddletown. Barry jumped off one way and the bike and Alan went the other. They picked themselves up, tidied and straightened the bike as best they could and proceeded to Dorchester. Shaken but not deterred, Alan passed the test!

At the time everyone maintained that taking a driving test in Dorchester, rather than in Bournemouth, was easier because there was less traffic and the examiners

Alan Mabey and his father in Heath Avenue with Alan's new bike.

were more tolerant of learner drivers and motor cyclists. Despite this popular belief, when the time came for me to take my test I went to Bournemouth on my Paloma moped. All went well until my chain came off half way round but luckily the examiner was out of sight at the time and I managed to fix it and get going again before he noticed, and yes, I passed first time.

On my seventeenth birthday there was a surprise waiting for me when I arrived home from work. There, in the garage, was a real motor bike, a 350 AJS with the registration number JJT933. Unbeknown to me Dad had done a deal with a friend of his who worked at Dardani and Large, the motorcycle dealers on Bournemouth Road. Dad drank with him in the Retreat pub up on hill and managed to buy the bike at a good price. The 'Ajay' was my pride and joy and I couldn't wait for my first run out on it. Later that night the boys called round for me and with a grin on my face from ear to ear we set of for my first ride on a proper bike!

We rode all evening going as far as Dorchester on long sweeping roads that were entirely new to me and I loved the feeling of speed and the freedom of the open road. On the run back home we went through Blandford and sped on to Wimborne. As it started to get dark we raced on through the long avenue of trees by Badbury Rings. Flushed by the glow of the lights on the speedometer and the two little side lights either side of the head light, that ride is a memory that has stayed with me forever.

Another friend from the railway was Ian McNulty who, like me, was always called 'Mac' which would confuse everyone! He lived in Layton Road, Upper Parkstone and rode a 500 Triumph Tiger 100 Twin. Some of us started to make regular trips to Swanage, mainly because we had become bored with just sitting in the Zebra Café in Poole High Street, near the Dolphin Hotel eating Miller's steak and kidney pies from

Picture below of Keith Sloper on his BSA Road Rocket.

the hot cabinet on the counter top. We preferred them covered with Heinz tomato ketchup and they were a real treat.

Our first attempt at finding a new place to hang out was to frequent Andy's Café in Wimborne but we had no luck with the local girls. Swanage, we thought, might be a better bet and oh, how right we were! My motorbike rides to Swanage were the start of a life long association with that small seaside town.

As our trips to Swanage became more frequent we got to know more local bikers and, importantly, local girls and we got on really well with most of them. We would hang out in the Playland Arcade, playing the juke box, and the penny machines, or in the Anchor Inn with its 'Sputnik' juke box. Very modern! Adam Faith was a favourite of Alan, but I loved Tell Laura I Love Her by Ricky Valance. We also became friendly with the Wareham boys and they were the best of all the local bikers for we would meet them on Wareham bridge and then race them to Swanage. Among those that I remember are Keith Sloper who had a wonderful Triumph Bonneville. Try as we could, none of could keep up with a machine of that quality, and Keith's riding skills were legendary!

There was also Lenny Gordon who had a beautiful black BSA Gold Flash, and Henry White who tragically died after hitting a tree on Nursery Bend. Another friend, Peter Walsh, was with him at the time but missed the tree and went straight into the field! Accidents were quite common amongst my biking friends. Ian McNulty hit a horse one dark foggy night at Harman's Cross as he was rushing back to Poole to work a night shift at the power station, where he was a painter. He had no gloves on and also did not wear a crash helmet. The horse was killed and Ian's Triumph Tiger 100 was a write off; it was picked up and taken to Triss Sharp's motor bike shop in Swanage. Ian was taken to Swanage Cottage Hospital and luckily survived the accident with only minor injuries

I always picked up Maurice Gale (or 'Woosty as he was known for some strange reason) at Sandford by the car auction garage. He never owned a bike and rode pillion to Swanage every night. The return trip was always exciting as Woosty often fell asleep by the time we reached Corfe Castle and had to be woken up on arrival at Sandford. Amazingly he never fell off the bike! On occasion we could be riding 'three up' as we always picked up some of the Wareham boys who'd also spent the evening in Swanage and were thumbing a lift home. Riding three up was really dodgy as I had to sit so far forward on the tank to make room for the extra person on the back! It never seemed to slow us down although the speed limit through Stoborough was always observed. We all tended to change down a gear outside the last house in the village for the blast across the causeway and the poor people in that house must have waited every night before they could go to sleep! We always stopped short of Wareham bridge in order to avoid getting caught in town. Late night petrol was available at the garage in West Street where you just had to knock and the old lady would get up and serve petrol across the pavement. You'd get a sorry look as you asked for half a gallon! Finally we always met up at Fleets Bridge roundabout to relieve ourselves, have a cigarette and a late night chat about conquests with the girls or how much beer had been consumed. Then we would go our separate ways and for me it was a quick dash up Old Wareham Road, down Haskells Road, into Livingstone Road and then into Churchill Road. Mum would have heard me coming from a long way off and would at last be able to relax and go to sleep!

Poole bikers at Stoney Down Cafe

Left to right: Martin Scott, Liz Langley, Dennis Lilly, David Scott, John Brown, Midge Holloway, Ray Dominey, John Mills, Derek Griffith.

Thanks to Midge Holloway for picture and names.

It was as this time (1961) that that I finally sold my beloved AJS and bought a 350 Matchless trials bike. I immediately joined the XHG Tigers Motorcycle Club with the intention of having a go at local trials meetings. John Walker, who worked in the stores at Huxham's, had talked me into this and the club met in an upstairs room at the Kings Arms pub near Wallisdown cross roads. My career as a triallist was short lived as I only entered two events, the first being at Bovington's army ranges and it was a disaster. It was very wet and muddy and the chain kept coming off my bike. I eventually retired from the competition and had to be rescued by Bob Foster's son who brought me home in the shop's van! The other trial was in the New Forest and was fantastic. It was held over the Perce Simon national course on Three Trees Hill and I did manage to finish it although I probably came last! Dad's friend, 'Uncle' Herbie came to watch, which I really did appreciate, and so did Ian Campbell who brought my new girl friend Vera with him. Although this second attempt at trialling was not as bad as the first, I decided it was not for me and called it a day after that. At the back of my mind was the thought that one day, when I was older, I would try again but I never did.

I loved my motor cycles and the freedom they gave me. The regular runs to Swanage were eventually to change my life for it was through these that I met the love of my life, Vera Weekes. We began going out together in 1959 and, four years later, on a wet Saturday morning on March 1963 we were married at Poole Registrar's

Office. We returned to Swanage for a small reception at Herston Hall and then left by steam train from Swanage station for a weekend in the Railway Hotel at Weymouth! We returned to a little one-bed flat in Canford Road, Tatnam, Poole, that we rented from one of Mum and Dad's friends, Dick Ridout. Dick was Herbie Bowden's brother in law and was a butcher in Tatnam. His shop had a newly converted flat above it which we rented for £3 a week and was a good place to start the rest of our lives together. No more rock and roll? No more motor bikes? Probably... or maybe not!

Myself, far right, with my friend Brian Schooling (white tie), at a dance at Oakdale Boys Club (probably '61/'62), local band from Hamworthy 'Bob and The KDC' were playing that night. Were you there?

Outside Vera's House, Swanage High Street, September 1960 On JJT933.

Chapter 6

AFTERWORD

This book attempts to recreate the experience of growing up in the post-war years, a period that now seems a very long time ago. In writing it I was struck by how little, despite the enormous social and technological changes that I've lived through, Terry and I have changed during a period of more than fifty years! Many aspects of our characters and the interests that we had when we were young have remained with us today.

An obvious example is our working lives. Although I have had a variety of jobs, it was my years as a railwayman that made the deepest impression on me and it was probably inevitable that as someone living in Swanage, I should eventually become involved with the town's steam railway. I began by volunteering as a cleaner, rising through the system to become a driver until, between 1996 and 2003, I was the Railway's full time (salaried) Operations Manager. Terry's grammar school education finally paid off for him. After almost twenty years in an office job at Parvalux Electric Motors in Wallisdown, he began studying for a degree with the newly established Open University. He then went on to achieve research degrees from the universities of Bristol and Southampton, and became a Senior Lecturer in history and politics at Southampton Solent University.

THE DECKCHAIRS L to R Steve Knowles, Hamish Murray, Paul McDonald, David Morgan, Frankie Rudd.

My love of rock and roll music never left me and, some thirty years after my enforced 'retirement', I joined a Swanage-based band called The Deckchairs. Just like the first time round I was lead singer and rhythm guitarist but I was no longer restricted to just the key of 'E' for I learned to play in all the keys. Rather surreally, when I needed help with a particular chord or sequence of chords, I would call Terry and be given an impromptu lesson in musical theory or guitar technique over the telephone! I sang and played with the Deckchairs for about ten years, between 1987 and 1997. Terry's own musical career never stopped and he played in several folk dance bands, including Diggory Venn, between 1988 and 2006. He is still a regular performer at local folk clubs and festivals as a solo singer-guitarist.

Another of our interests that re-surfaced in the early 1980s was running. I became Hamworthy Engineering's cross country champion while Terry re-joined Bournemouth Athletic Club when his eldest son took up the sport as a twelve year old. He competed in the 'veterans' category in cross country and road races but soon realised he was still, at heart, the half-miler he had been in his late teens and early twenties.

Just as my love of music has never left me, my love for motorbikes has remained strong and I have almost always had a motor bike. I have owned a variety of machines including some quite powerful ones such as a Triton which is a combined Triumph and Norton, both great names from Britain's motorcycling history, and the 'dream bike' of many a 'wannabe' café-racer of my youth, a BSA Gold Star. Most recently, I painstakingly recreated my beloved Matchless 350 trials bike that I owned in the early sixties.

One final point is that our childhood dream of visiting Newfoundland and meeting our many relatives there eventually came true, but not until we were in our late fifties. We have now become firm friends with our first cousins, one of whom now lives in Halifax, Nova Scotia, while another still lives in Grand Falls, our father's home town.

Neither of us has lived in Upper Parkstone since the 1960s but recently experienced a sense of déjà vu. Until quite recently all three of Terry's sons lived in Upper Parkstone and at a birthday party for one of his grandchildren we realised that his oldest son's house in Vale Road was next door to the one where Dad had lassoed the tree! Its front garden now seemed ridiculously small! The idea of a quite tall tree standing on that tiny plot of land seemed impossible but we checked with 'Auntie Barbara' and she confirmed that it was indeed her mother's house. We had a similar experience when we went to a Christmas fete at Courthill School where one of Terry's grandchildren was soon to become a pupil. We wandered all around the buildings, working out where our classrooms had been. Again, it seemed so small.

Upper Parkstone is still one of Poole's most diverse suburbs and, as far as we can see, most of the buildings (with the obvious exceptions of the Regal cinema and the Retreat public house) are still there. The great majority, though, are now used for different purposes. Yet to those of us who grew up there in the post-war years, it remains a familiar place. It's just so much busier and more crowded than it used to be!

Paul's BSA Gold Star.

Paul McDonald - Ian McNulty - ? - Alan Mabey - Ian Campbell
Westover Road, Bournemouth.

Index

87